CUSTOMER PERSUASION

How to Influence Your Customers to Buy More & Why an Ethical Approach Will Always Win

CHLOË THOMAS

Kernu Publishing

© Chloë Thomas

Originally published 2016

Kernu Publishing

PO Box 740

Truro

Cornwall

TR1 9HE

United Kingdom

All rights reserved. Apart from limited use for private study, teaching, research, criticism or review, no part of this publication may be reproduced, stored or transmitted without the prior permission in writing of the copyright owner and publisher of this book.

Praise for Customer Persuasion

If you don't have a pen and paper ready you'll be scrambling for one inside a few paragraphs. Chloë Thomas's encyclopaedic knowledge of eCommerce businesses around the world, together with real-life examples of how to manipulate your website visitors make this a must for your e-commerce self-development!

Pascal Culverhouse, Founder & Managing Director, The Electric Tobacconist Ltd & LLC, electrictobacconist.co.uk

Chloë has once again done what she does best and distilled the knowledge of professionals into a MasterPlan guide that a small business owner can not only understand but can implement to grow their business.

You'll find no complicated jargon in Customer Persuasion, instead Chloë walks you through the customer journey step by step from the initial step of attracting the right visitors to your website stage by stage to converting them into repeat customers. Throughout the book you'll find real life examples to illustrate the steps you need to take to turn your visitors into first time buyers, then into repeat buyers and finally into regular customers.

While Chloë has tailored the book for small businesses, even the largest retailers should be reading Customer Persuasion. Everything you need to know is distilled down into a simple framework that's easy to follow and will help accelerate the growth of your business.

Chris Dawson, Editor, Tamebay tamebay.com

In the age of the customer, Customer Persuasion is an invaluable resource for any brand – whether just starting out or struggling to move towards a customer-centric business model.

The book is packed with easy-to-follow, actionable advice to aid companies in understanding how to earn their customers' interest, foster it, keep it and capitalise on it.

Skip Fidura, Client Services Director, dotmailer, dotmailer.com

Once again Chloë has delivered a book aimed at the smaller business which talks in a language you can understand and, just as importantly, apply to your business. Industry jargon is explained but also applied in a way that you can work with rather than get bogged down in. It's just packed full of ideas and action points but with an overall strategy for getting your business working online. Even if, like me, you run an established business this book is worth reading because it will remind you of what you should be doing, and maybe even a few things you didn't know you should.

Dominic Irons, Owner, Bureau Direct, www.bureaudirect.co.uk

In a world heavy on jargon, insider knowledge and almost infinite options it is difficult to pull together an end to end methodology. Chloe Thomas takes a straight forward step by step approach to creating the Customer MasterPlan. Written in digestible pieces this walk through of the customer journey from awareness to repeat purchase demystifies the process and enables the reader with practical information and measurements that makes sense of it all.

Jason Smith, Bazaarvoice

Customer Persuasion: How to grow your business and make your customers happy is a really nice introduction into the customer centric world of eCommerce. It provides a sensible, easy to follow template for new business owners and seasoned online professionals alike.

What I like most about the book, is that it's not full of "marketing jargon' and is therefore extremely easy to follow and put into practice. It is also packed with stacks of real life examples that market leading companies are successfully putting into practice for the reader to draw inspiration from.

A cracking read!

Zak Edwards, Managing Director, Prezzybox.com

A compendious overview of the selling processes online, all from the position of an ethical and authentic connection with the customer. This book is both a glossary of all of the digital marketing terms you'll come across and a practical, illustrated guide of these techniques in practice – rolled up in an accessible style.

Ian Jindal, Editor, Internet Retailing

Chloë has condensed the options, strategies and tactics to ensure ones product or service will reach the maximum amount of prospects, turn them into fans and then customers. eCommerce has evolved so much in the past few years, that to ignore this blueprint will leave you in the wake of your competitors and more importantly alienate prospects, who have a high expectation of what we do to turn them into customers. Thank you Chloë, another epic book.

We also love the fact that there are great insights into the subscription model that ensure the nurture and expectation are fully understood and the murky world of analytics now makes sense.

Sebastian Galbraith-Helps, Chief Bee, HoneyTreeBespoke.com

Chloë's latest book is a triumph, it guides you through the journey of finding your audience and creating a strong customer base. What's different about Chloë's book is that it never loses focus on the customer perspective. It tells you how to make sure customers understand your proposition and is jammed full of useful examples that are easy to follow. I'd recommend it to anyone that wants to take their business to the next level.

Alex O'Byrne, Founding Director, We Make Websites, wemakewebsites.com

There is something refreshingly honest in the opening pages of Chloë's latest book: "All marketing is a form of manipulation", it's also great to see ethics included right up there in the title. We could all lie to our customers to get them in the door, but instead what Chloë has done here is give us a comprehensive ecommerce to-do list of customer-friendly actions. I challenge any company to say they have ticked every box! It's not just general theory, it is practical and actionable, things like "look at this specific data in analytics, then do something". The book doesn't try to give a one-size-fits-all answer to your problems, it guides you through how to find out what's right for your business. I guarantee you'll be sticking post-it notes in this book of things to investigate further, I know I will.

As Chloë rightly points out, customer expectations have increased, retailers need to meet or exceed that expectation if they are to persuade their visitors to become customers. The internet has made it easier for customers to exercise choice in whom they purchase from, they vote with their feet and force us to raise the bar, (so who is manipulating who?!) simply having a website is not enough.

So whether you're a small ecommerce company wanting to get big or a big company wondering what they've missed, this book will be a great help. Its flow is logical and it is comprehensive, it makes you appreciate how many factors go in to successful ecommerce.

Stuart McMillan Deputy Head of Ecommerce, Schuh.co.uk

Contents

Chapter 1: Why Customer Persuasion?   **11**

Customer service must now be omnipresent; There's no model out there to help you; New challenges to deal with; Beware of the Bright Shiny Object; Customers are online-savvy; Increasing competition between online businesses; Excess of marketing choices

Chapter 2: Introducing The Customer MasterPlan   **21**

Customer Lifetime Value; RFM; The Customer MasterPlan model; The Levels; Why it's important; The Conversation; Subscription businesses; One time purchase businesses; For start-ups; For established businesses; Structure of this book

Chapter 3: Introducing The Conversation   **37**

What is The Conversation; It's about what you say and what you do; Customer Generated Content; Content generated by other influencers; How your customers feel; Why do you need to think about The Conversation?; How do you improve The Conversation's ability to build trust?; Keeping The Conversation consistent; The Editorial Mission Statement; The Customer Voice word cloud

Chapter 4: Stage 1: Attracting the Right Visitors   **55**

The aim of Stage 1; Where does the social media follower fit in?; How The Conversation fits in; What to learn from my existing customers; Researching what you should do and say; Customer surveys; Google Analytics benchmarking; Competitor analysis; Marketing actions; Shine a Light; Target customers; Get found; Website actions including SEO tweaks

Chapter 5: Stage 2: Turning Visitors into Enquirers   **97**

The aim of Stage 2; Strange things happen in Stage 2; How The Conversation fits in; What to learn from my existing customers; Researching where to focus your effort; Building The Conversation; Trust marks and Guarantees; Adding longer customer generated content; The About Us page; Website actions to obtain email addresses; Pop-ups and incentives; Getting email sign ups from places other than your website; Marketing actions; Brand awareness; Remarketing

Chapter 6: Stage 3: Turning Enquirers into First Time Buyers   **147**

The aim of Stage 3; How the Conversation fits in; What to learn from my existing customers; What products to promote; Checkout funnels; Conversion rate optimisation; User testing; Researching what customers want; Website actions; Split testing; Searchandising; Product information that's not on the product pages; Customer personas; Customer generated content and social proof; Product actions and product pages; Customer service actions; Marketing actions; Welcome sequences; Abandoned basket reminders; Remarketing; A warning about promotions

Chapter 7: Stage 4: Creating Repeat Buyers   **195**

The aim of Stage 4; How the Conversation fits in; What to learn from my existing customers; Customer service actions; The parcel; Dealing with complaints; Product selection and quality; Marketing actions; Direct communication campaigns; Post purchase sequences; Anniversary of first purchase campaigns; Reactivation campaigns; The dangers of personalised emails; Remarketing

Chapter 8: Stage 5: Turning Repeat Buyers into Regular Buyers   **217**

The aim of Stage 5; How the Conversation fits in; What to learn from my existing customers; Marketing actions; Customer communities; Brand advocates; Mobile apps

Chapter 9: Where to Start   **231**

Advice for start-ups; Advice for established businesses; How to work out which is your weakest Stage; Free resources to help you

Glossary   **243**
About the Author   **245**
The eCommerce MasterPlan Podcast   **247**
Other books   **249**

1 Why Customer Persuasion?

A TIPPING point has been reached in marketing, a point where businesses have soooo many marketing options that it often leads to paralysis.

Not only are businesses struggling to work out what they should be doing to attract new customers and keep their existing customers coming back, customers are demanding and expecting more than ever.

Online competition is also increasing, leading to ever-lower returns on investment for businesses who don't adapt their marketing to put it in front of the right people, or cut through all the noise created by the competition.

All of this means marketing has to be top notch – the right message, to the right person, at the right time, AND it has to be a powerful message that cuts through all the noise and gets the customer to do something.

All marketing is a form of manipulation, an act of persuasion. To succeed, you now need to acknowledge that and learn how to persuade customers really efficiently, in order to make them happy and grow your businesses.

Once you've learnt the methods of persuasion you can use them in a positive or unscrupulous way. But if you run your business in an unscrupulous way, you're going to get into difficulties really quickly. Customers are now too clever; they'll sniff you out and you'll suffer the consequences.

For me, persuasion in marketing is all about using your marketing skills in a clever way to get the right outcome for your business and your customer.

The right marketing method has to be chosen and the right message put out there, all done cohesively to give the customer the all-round experience that they're looking for.

Therefore, to persuade successfully you need to:

- Listen to your customers and learn what's important to them.
- Understand the Stage they are at in their relationship with your business.
- Choose the marketing that will get the customers to respond.
- Craft the messages that will have the biggest impact on your customers.
- Listen to your customers so you can continue to give them more of what they want.

Customer service must now be omnipresent

This book is not just about improving your marketing.

The other big shift that's been happening in business is that customers are no longer king. They are now autocratic emperors who can only be satisfied by a company building everything around them. This means that customer service must now be omnipresent.

Customer service should be considered in every part of the business, not just in the call centre or by Janet who answers the phones. It has to be a consideration in finance, HR, the warehouse, marketing, IT – every single person in a business must be focused on the customer. Every single decision made in the business should be made by taking into account what the customer needs.

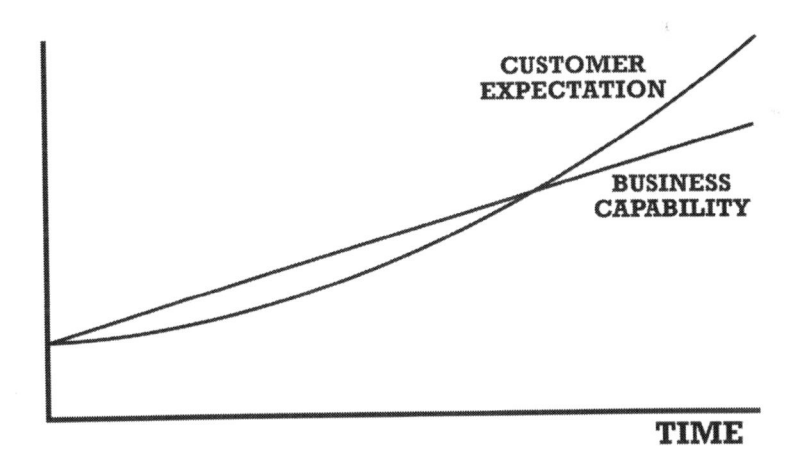

[Graph showing two upward curves over TIME, labelled CUSTOMER EXPECTATION (steeper) and BUSINESS CAPABILITY]

This is because customer expectations are now increasing faster than a traditional business increases its capability, which makes it much harder to keep the customer happy and buying from you.

Putting the customer at the heart of the business is not easy. Larger businesses often dedicate years to making this switch, putting most of the effort into getting the team to change their mindset.

House of Fraser (houseoffraser.co.uk) spent three years changing things around, with key actions being:

- Merging the brand, CRM and multichannel teams under one "Chief Customer Officer".
- Changing the business' thinking from:
    - Revenue by Channel to Revenue by Customer.
    - Channel Centric (mobile, store, web, app, etc.) to Customer Centric.

Serious Readers (seriousreaders.com) now base the whole of their business on the KPI of how many raving fans they have.[1]

ASOS (asos.com) attributes their success over the last 15 years to "Following the Customer" – working out what the customer wants and building it for them.

Some of these points make it seem very simple, and for the smaller business, it's a lot easier than for bigger companies. There are fewer people to change, things happen more quickly, everyone is closer to the customer and can witness the results first-hand.

---

[1] If you'd like to hear more about this you can listen to my interview with founder Alex Pratt at: eCommerceMasterPlan.com/Podcast

However, whilst it might be easier, it's still not that easy and you will have to work at it. Here are three simple things you can do to improve how you look after your customers:

- Listen. That might be as simple as looking at what they're buying, which pages they're visiting on the website, and checking in on customer service calls. I'll cover lots of ways to do this as I work through the Stages of The Customer MasterPlan.
- Never assume you know what they want.
- Make sure everyone in the team is learning and focusing on what the customer wants.

There's no model out there to help you

Right now, there is no model out there designed to help you deal with these realities, to help you mitigate the obstacles and take advantage of the available opportunities.

Dealing with these challenges requires a change of approach and a change of mindset. You need to know how to harness the power of your customers and use a greater understanding of how they progress through your business, in order to identify the right marketing and messages to use at each Stage of that journey.

To grow a business, the marketing choices must be made in a new way and you need to treat the customer in a new way.

There are a lot of models out there that help with parts of these challenges, but none can bring it all together in a practical, easy to follow, easy to remember model, enabling the quick decision-making you need.

That's what the rest of this book is going to outline for you, bringing together two key concepts into one simple-to-follow model:

- The power of The Conversation.
- The 5 Stages of The Customer MasterPlan.

New challenges to deal with

There are three realities which converge to make The Customer MasterPlan a necessary approach for any business that wants to succeed:

- Customers are now much more savvy online than they were ten (or even five!) years ago.
- Huge growth in online businesses means more competition between those businesses.
- There are too many marketing choices. It's no longer a choice of email or direct mail, there are now hundreds of options and new ones emerging every week.

This means that it's both harder and more important than ever to make the right marketing decisions.

It also means that to be successful, you need to take a different approach to your marketing.

I speak to hundreds of business owners and marketers every year. The most successful are those who've worked out what their customer wants, AND how to deliver that to them. They've found the right marketing mix.

Often, that's just one or two marketing methods executed well (and not necessarily perfectly – there's usually still plenty of room for improvement). It is not doing lots of different things.

But, there are many, many marketing options to choose from. So the successful ones are those who can find the right options fastest, realise they've found a good one, and stick with it.

Of course, it takes time to test and optimise each method to find out what works for you. It is also important to understand that what works this month might not work as well next month.

Beware of the 'Bright Shiny Object'

A "Bright Shiny Object" is that exciting, new marketing tool which you hear about at a conference or arrives in your inbox, and is so fresh and exciting that it entirely distracts you from the challenge already at hand.

Maybe you need more traffic to the website, and you see a great presentation on some new abandoned basket software – it's not going to get you more traffic, but wow is it interesting! So you spend the next three weeks and hundreds of pounds implementing it in the business. Sure, it increases conversion rate by 30%, but that's only an extra 10 orders a month and you've still not fixed the initial traffic need.

That is the danger of the Bright Shiny Object.

To succeed nowadays, it's important to pick the right marketing method for each objective you want to achieve. So isolate the objective first, and then find the right marketing method to meet that objective in your business.

The customers are online-savvy

More than 1 in 4 UK residents (28%) buy online at least once a week, and 73% buy online several times a month.[2]

74% of SME e-retailers increased their sales in 2015, the highest level of the last three years (2014 = 58%, 2013 = 49%).[3]

It is now the norm for people to buy online regularly, not the exception. And the more often they buy, the more they get used to the process and the more they are willing to spend, in value and frequency.

Great news because it's leading to a growth in online sales across the board. However, the customers are judging you against everyone else they buy from – their supermarket, Amazon, eBay, and more. You have to deliver what they expect.

Increase in competition between online businesses

53% of SME e-retailers claim that competition was more intense in 2015, the highest ever level of competition reported.[4] This intensity is predominantly coming from:

- On the move smartphone shopping – 47% of e-retailers feel this is increasing competition for them.
- Price promotions encouraging customers to look out for the best deals – 44%.
- Consumer price sensitivity – 52%.
- Increased number of websites – 52%.

---

2   "The UK Customer Service and Support Market", eDigitalResearch iAdvize report, September 2015.
3   Royal Mail's annual tracker study into UK SME e-retailers. 2015.
4   Royal Mail's annual tracker study into UK SME e-retailers. 2015.

The greater the competition (whether from other online retailers in your country, overseas, or offline), the stronger your marketing must be to get the customer to pick you, not anyone else, and to make sure those who are perfect for you can find you.

Excess of marketing choices

To deal with increased competition, 7 in 10 SME e-retailers are planning on increasing the number of channels they sell through in 2016, including 85% who are planning on selling through an additional online marketplace.[5]

Not only are there more options than ever before, consumers are more savvy than ever before and there is more competition than ever before. This means the marketing has to be executed well, with the right message at the right time to the right consumer.

To overcome these challenges, it's first necessary to work out the issue or opportunity that needs to be solved, and then find the marketing method that will deliver it.

Customer Persuasion

For all those reasons we need to embrace the fact that we manipulate customers in order to make our businesses successful and our customers happy.

Through the rest of this book I'll outline how to do this, using two concepts The Conversation and The Customer MasterPlan.

---

[5] Royal Mail's annual tracker study into UK SME e-retailers, 2015.

Together they will...

- Help your business find the right marketing methods to solve your problems.
- Help you understand your customers better.
- Help your business work out the messages to put in front of your customers.

Marketing is at a tipping point, and this book will guide you into the new reality.

If you're reading this in 2016, you have the opportunity to get ahead of the pack and create a real competitive advantage for your business.

If you're reading this book after 2016, in many industries you will still be able to use it to get ahead of the pack. If your competitors are already great at listening to the customer and planning the best marketing strategy, then this is going to your quickest way to catch up.

Want to find out exactly what it's all about? Read on!

2 Introducing The Customer MasterPlan

THE CUSTOMER MasterPlan is a model I've designed and worked on over the last few years, enabling smaller businesses to cut through the plethora of options and make the right decision about what they should do next. It's about making better decisions faster, so you can grow your business faster and more efficiently.

In designing it, I've incorporated many existing concepts (such as RFM and CLV) and marketing theories from many different industries. I've discussed marketing with many business owners and marketers, I've attended conferences, read reports and case studies and books, listened to podcasts, and watched videos and attended shows.

I've distilled all this research down into a simple framework that's easy to follow, will stand the test of time, and will enable you to speed up the growth of your business.

There are lots of things happening in the world that make successfully marketing and growing any business hard. There are so many things you could do that it's hard to find the one that's going to work. It's very easy to get distracted by those bright shiny objects and forget about the successful marketing you've already been doing. The world is also a lot more competitive – there are more businesses out there and it's become much easier for customers to shop around. Finally, the customers are expecting more and are skilled in getting the best result for themselves.

At the core of the model is getting to understand your customers better than you ever have before, using this knowledge to deliver what they want and encouraging them to buy as much as possible (so basically, the whole model is a way to manipulate the results you want to see). This should all be carried out whilst treating the customers with the utmost of respect. If you don't, you'll run into problems very quickly.

Two important concepts to start with

CLV: Customer Lifetime Value

Every business should be looking to improve its CLV, the worth of a customer over their whole lifetime. Focusing on CLV should remind a business to market to both new and existing customers, and build a relationship with those customers.

Too often, calculating CLV is a nightmare (or impossible!) and becomes the focus of the project, or it becomes a tool to justify customer incentives and discounts – which is the exact opposite of what it should be about!

The reason it doesn't tend to work is that it's such a complex calculation. Whilst the concept of CLV, of "increasing the value and strength of the customer's relationship with you in order to sell them more," is intrinsic, I am not expecting any of you to actually try to work it out as a specific value.[6]

Embrace CLV as a concept, but not as a number.

RFM: Recency, Frequency, Monetary Value

It's a concept from the good old days of mail order catalogue retailing, where it still underpins data selection to this day (rightly so, as it's a very good model). Back when I managed the catalogue mailings at UK multichannel business Past Times in the mid-2000s, it was my bread and butter.

RFM is a simple way of segmenting your list of buyers to understand how good your list is and market to the list more effectively. RFM involves segmenting the list using three criteria:

- Recency: how long it's been since the customer's last purchase.
- Frequency: how many times the customer has bought from you during their whole relationship with your business.
- Monetary Value: how much the customer spends with you in each transaction, usually as an average.

A simple RFM segmentation grid might look like this (with each white cell showing how many customers fit into that segment). Although the price breaks may shift for different businesses, the time spans are usually six-month windows.

---

[6] Although should you want to, there is a simple guide in my first book *eCommerce MasterPlan: Your 3 Steps to Successful Online Selling*. You can find it in Chapter 9.

Only purchased once

Last Order> AOV	0-6m	7-12m	13-18m	19-24m	25-36m	37-42m	42m+
£0-30							
£30-60							
£60-100							
£100+							

Purchased twice

Last Order> AOV	0-6m	7-12m	13-18m	19-24m	25-36m	37-42m	42m+
£0-30							
£30-60							
£60-100							
£100+							

Purchased three times

Last Order> AOV	0-6m	7-12m	13-18m	19-24m	25-36m	37-42m	42m+
£0-30							
£30-60							
£60-100							
£100+							

Purchased more than three times

Last Order> AOV	0-6m	7-12m	13-18m	19-24m	25-36m	37-42m	42m+
£0-30							
£30-60							
£60-100							
£100+							

Using this you can quickly see your best customers – in this example those who have:

- Recency = Ordered in the last six months.
- Frequency = Ordered more than three times.
- Monetary value = Average Order Value (AOV) over £100.

When selecting data for marketing or working on your marketing plans, R, F, and M are not equally important. The general feeling is that the most important factor is recency, then frequency, then monetary value.

At no point during this book am I going to suggest you build an RFM model of your data (it's a very time-consuming process, especially the first time you do it). But I will be taking these principles into The Customer MasterPlan model.

Recency is going to be part of every Stage in the model, so always think about how fast you can get the right marketing message to someone who's just interacted with a business, and how the message changes if they fail to respond.

Frequency (as you'll see below) is built into the model itself with the Repeat Buyer and Regular Buyer levels.

Monetary value won't be covered a lot, as it's the least important metric, but I will be talking about price points and average order values (AOVs) where relevant.

Throughout the coming chapters I won't be making specific reference to these concepts again, but I think it's useful for you to be aware that they are fundamental building blocks.

Introducing The Customer MasterPlan

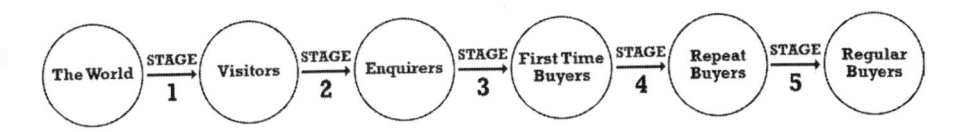

The World → STAGE 1 → Visitors → STAGE 2 → Enquirers → STAGE 3 → First Time Buyers → STAGE 4 → Repeat Buyers → STAGE 5 → Regular Buyers

Here it is – the core of The Customer MasterPlan model.

This is how to achieve eCommerce business success in six circles and five arrows!

It really is.

Your sole responsibility in growing your eCommerce business (or any business) is to get as many people from the left-hand side onto the right-hand side. Turning people who don't know you exist into Regular Buyers.

	Change people from:	To:	How?
Stage 1	The World *Unknown customers*	Visitor	Make the world aware your products, services and business exist (or a segment of the world). Get the interested people to visit you.
Stage 2	Visitor *Unknown potential customer*	Enquirer	Get those interested people to leave you with an email address so they become an "Enquirer".
Stage 3	Enquirer *Known potential customer*	First Time Buyer	Convert your Enquirers into First Time Buyers.
Stage 4	First Time Buyer *Known customer*	Repeat Buyer	Once they've bought once, you want to get them to buy again. They're not a real buyer until they've bought multiple times!
Stage 5	Repeat Buyer *Known fan*	Regular Buyer *Known Advocate*	Then (for the icing on the cake) you want to build a strong relationship with them so that you can rely on them buying from you on a regular basis.

That's it.

That is how to be successful in eCommerce.

Of course, people will leapfrog some Stages, most often in the process of becoming a First Time Buyer. And that's OK – it just means your marketing is working really well.

Industry theories and case studies repeatedly show that if you follow this model your business will grow faster.

Thinking of your business in this structure also makes it really straightforward to work out where you're under-performing – which Stage isn't doing what it should? (You will find out how to work that out in Chapter 9.) Each Stage requires a different message and a different set of actions, and I have a chapter on each one to help you work out how to improve things.

The great news is that each time you improve one Stage, the whole model improves!

In the book, I'll be referring to all humans as "customers". As they travel from left to right, a business gets to know them a little better.

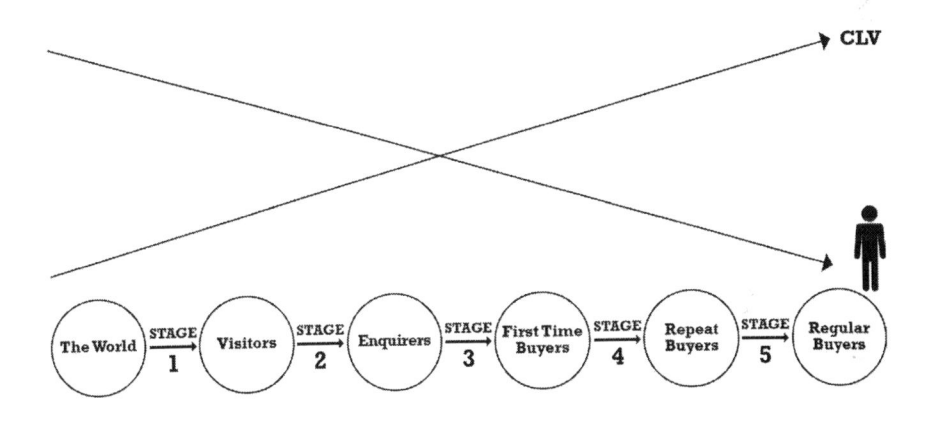

```
The World →STAGE 1→ Visitors →STAGE 2→ Enquirers →STAGE 3→ First Time Buyers →STAGE 4→ Repeat Buyers →STAGE 5→ Regular Buyers    CLV
```

Other factors to consider

As you move customers along The MasterPlan, they'll become more valuable to you – their CLV will increase.

BUT at each Stage of The Customer MasterPlan, you have fewer and fewer customers to market to.

The different audience sizes at each Stage and the level of potential CLV at each Stage has an impact on the marketing you should employ. I've taken that into account throughout the book.

For example, Blue Chip Wrestling (bluechipwrestling.com) in the USA are big fans of giving things away to encourage customers to come back and buy. They give gifts away when someone becomes an Enquirer, and when someone buys from them. But the gifts have very different costs and postage costs:

- New Enquirers get a bumper sticker.
- First Time Buyers get a free t-shirt.

Introducing the last part of The Customer MasterPlan model: The Conversation

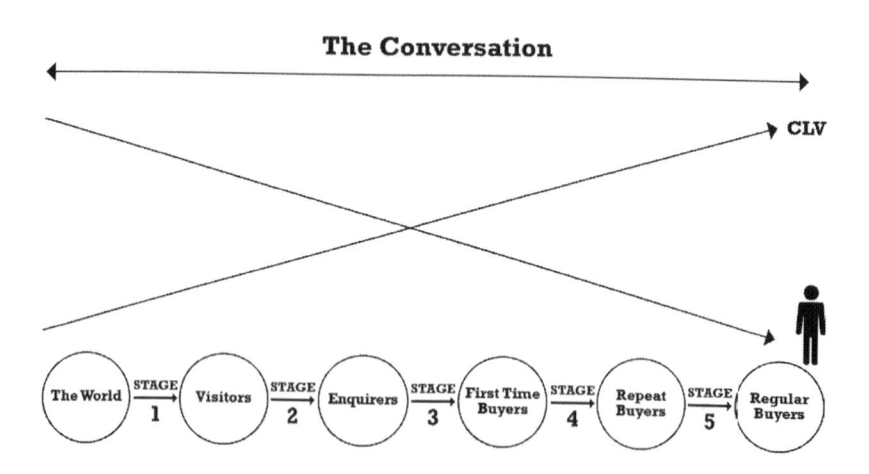

The Conversation

CLV

The World → STAGE 1 → Visitors → STAGE 2 → Enquirers → STAGE 3 → First Time Buyers → STAGE 4 → Repeat Buyers → STAGE 5 → Regular Buyers

You may be wondering why on earth Blue Chip Wrestling would give freebies to every Buyer, let alone every Enquirer.

Well, that's where the third part of the model comes in – The Conversation.

The Customer MasterPlan model is not about one-hit-wonder marketing; it's about building a consistent communication program with customers. From the point where they are out in the world and first hear about you, right through to the point they've started buying every month, should be one continuous Conversation.

It's a Conversation that crosses channels, involves other people (other customers, magazines, newspapers), and involves experiences you will never even hear anything about.

It's a Conversation that needs to paint a consistent picture of your business. The elements of it that you have control over should always look and feel like your brand, and that consistency will mean the parts you don't have control over should feel like your brand too.

This Conversation needs to be built to speed up how fast customers go from Visitor to Enquirer, and from Enquirer to First Time Buyer, because that's a great way to increase your profitability.

The timing of when marketing happens has a role to play in this (think back to the power of Recency in RFM above), but The Conversation has an even bigger role to play.

The importance of The Conversation is its role in building trust between your business and the customers who are interacting with it. You need to create a relationship with them – because that's what trust is all about, and people buy from businesses they trust.

Don't worry if this concept feels a bit out-there, or overwhelming and complex at the moment. I'll explain more about it in

Chapter 3 and I'll be frequently explaining how to build it as I go through each Stage of the model.

Special cases

There are a couple of types of eCommerce business where The Customer MasterPlan model needs to be adapted...

Subscription businesses

You still have to get your customers through every Stage of the model. You can think of it like:

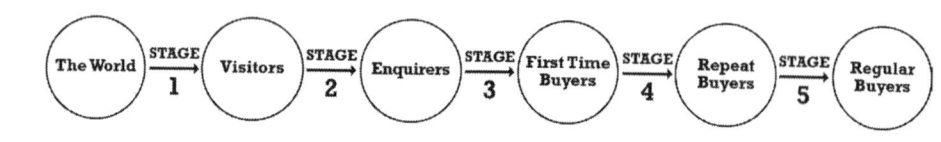

The World → STAGE 1 → Visitors → STAGE 2 → Enquirers → STAGE 3 → First Time Buyers → STAGE 4 → Repeat Buyers → STAGE 5 → Regular Buyers

	Change people from:	To:	How?
Stage 1	The World *Unknown customers*	Visitor	Make the world aware your products, services and business exist (or a segment of the world). Get the interested customers to visit you.
Stage 2	Visitor *Unknown potential customer*	Enquirer	Get those interested customers to leave you with an email address so they become an "Enquirer".
Stage 3	Enquirer *Known potential customer*	First Time Buyer	Convert your Enquirers into Buyers of your subscription.
Stage 4	First Time Buyer *Known customer*	Repeat Buyer	This is their first period of subscription. During this first month/quarter/week, you need to make sure they don't cancel — remember, they're not a real customer until they've bought multiple times! This is a set period of time until the chance of cancelling drops off.
Stage 5	Repeat Buyer *Known fan*	Regular Buyer *Known Advocate*	If someone gets to the point where the chance of cancelling is remote or negligible, then they are a true subscriber.

This theory frequently plays out in the recruitment marketing of the big subscription businesses.

Introducing The Customer MasterPlan | 31

Here's a recent leaflet from Abel and Cole (vegetable box deliveries), where they are trying to get someone not just to have one box, but to get past the fourth box:

It's a complex offer.

- 1st box = 50% off
- 2nd box = full price
- 3rd box = full price
- 4th box = 50% off and a free gift

It's clearly worth the complexity for them to make sure they're getting a subscriber (Regular Buyer) from their marketing, not just a First Time Buyer.

One-time purchase businesses

In some businesses there is very little chance of repeat purchase, or the repeat purchase cycle is so long that it's unlikely a customer wants to hear from you in the meantime.

Here are two examples:

- Turtle Mat (turtlemat.co.uk) makes the world's best doormats. Each one comes with a five-year guarantee – so they don't often need replacing, and not many people have multiple doors that require doormats! They might get a second purchase, but no one is going to turn into a Regular Buyer.

- Goodbye Crutches (goodbyecrutches.com) sells alternatives to crutches for people who currently require them. Fundamentally, they don't want their customers to ever need them again! But they might get a second purchase if someone sees enough value in the products that they want a second option.

Essentially, this type of business should follow the same model, but with a couple of tweaks:

1. The point of profitable marketing needs to come sooner! In fact, unlike most eCommerce businesses, the First Time Buyer Stage needs to be profitable.

2. The advocacy part needs to happen at the First Time Buyer point, because you want them to recommend you the next time they meet someone with the problem you solve.

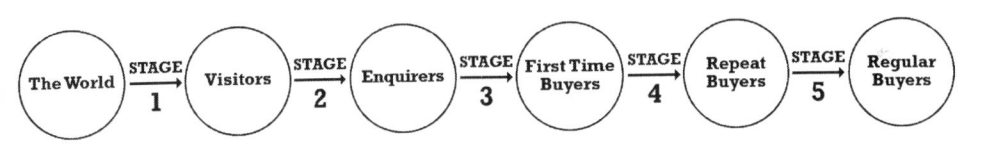

The World → STAGE 1 → Visitors → STAGE 2 → Enquirers → STAGE 3 → First Time Buyers → STAGE 4 → Repeat Buyers → STAGE 5 → Regular Buyers

	Change people from:	To:	How?
Stage 1	The World *Unknown customers*	Visitor	Make the world aware your products, services and business exist (or a segment of the world). Get the interested people to visit you.
Stage 2	Visitor *Unknown potential customer*	Enquirer	Get those interested people to leave you with an email address so they become an "Enquirer".
Stage 3	Enquirer *Known potential customer*	First Time Buyer	Convert your Enquirers into First Time Buyers.
Stage 4	First Time Buyer *Known customer*	Repeat Buyer	In this Stage you should be making sure you pick up any second order, if there's potential for it. BUT your main aim is to treat them so well that they won't hesitate to rave about your product.
Stage 5	Repeat Buyer *Known fan*	Regular Buyer *Known Advocate*	Does not apply. BUT some of the methods in this Stage will help you drive referrals.

Does The Customer MasterPlan work equally well for start-ups and established businesses?

Yes.

However, the implementation approach will vary between them.

Start-ups

Read the whole book and get to grips with the concepts.

Before you launch, get the basics of Stage 1, 2 and 3 in place:

- **Stage 1:** What marketing you're going to test to build awareness.
- **Stage 2:** Email sign up in place.
- **Stage 3:** A simple "Welcome" program to encourage the purchase.

(Of course, if you want to do more on those Stages before you launch then go for it! But don't use getting it perfect as an excuse to delay getting started.)

Then watch your performance stats and volumes, and as the model fills up with customers, work on the next area that needs to be improved. For example, if you're getting lots of First Time Buyers, it's time to work on Stage 4. If you're getting lots of Enquirers but they're not converting, you need to do more work on Stage 3.

Established businesses

Read the whole book and get to grips with the concepts.

Before you dive in, work through Chapter 9 to identify where you should start.

Look at all the options for the stage you are tackling and implement a couple of things that you don't currently do, or improve on the areas you feel are the weakest.

Then re-measure and work on the Stage that is now the weakest.

Remember, this is a process of continuous optimisation that will last forever!

Often for an established business, the first challenge will be to understand which parts of your current marketing strategy fit with which Stage, and getting all that split out so you can see what's happening throughout your Customer MasterPlan.

The structure of this book

Hopefully, this quick run through of the model means you can see how it's going to help deploy your resources and identify the right things to be doing at each Stage.

In the following chapters, I'll be covering:

- A whole chapter on the power of The Conversation and how you can build trust with your customers.
- Five chapters on the model – one for each Stage, including:
    - Marketing actions.
    - Website actions.
    - Customer service actions.
    - Product actions.
    - Examples, case studies, and much more.

- The last practical "What to Do" section will show you how to work out which Stage you should start with, to get the greatest impact fastest.

There are a number of resources on the website to help you, including:

- A workbook you can use to manage your improvements.
- A checklist for each chapter.

Those are available for free at eCommerceMasterPlan.com/free

Let's get started!

3 Introducing The Conversation

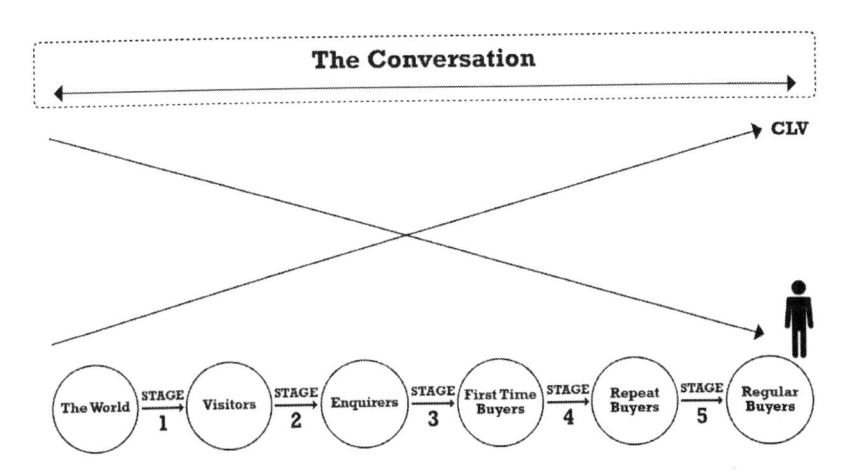

The Conversation

```
The World →STAGE 1→ Visitors →STAGE 2→ Enquirers →STAGE 3→ First Time Buyers →STAGE 4→ Repeat Buyers →STAGE 5→ Regular Buyers → CLV
```

THE CONVERSATION stretches across the whole model. From getting the world to take notice of you and visit your site, right through to getting a customer to buy repeatedly from you.

Blacker Yarns (blackeryarns.co.uk) are the retail side of a UK wool mill, specialising in the wool of rare and traditional breed sheep. Sue Blacker runs her team to have a complete focus on the provenance of the wool (where the wool came from – sheep breed and location) and the quality of the product. They are also heavily focused on the customer experience – The Conversation.

Sue's run lots of surveys and spoken to her customers to understand that, for them, the key is the provenance and what inspired it. For example, in 2015 they celebrated their first ten years in business and launched a special 10th anniversary yarn, inspired by the mining heritage of Cornwall (the UK county they are based in).

They understand that their customers prefer to feel the wool before committing to purchase enough to knit a garment. Online, they use photography, words, and icons to help convey the quality of each yarn. In order to provide the real touch experience, they've expanded their network of stockists so that customers can get their hands on a ball of yarn and test it out – see how it knits.

Most knitters and crocheters will buy one ball before committing to enough for a whole project. So Sue and her team have packed both sides of the paper band that goes around the wool with detailed information about their products, as well as the all-important call to action (CTA). This makes it super easy for the customer to find more of a wool they like. Sue and her team at Blacker Yarns understand how The Conversation with their customer unfolds and the messages it needs to contain. They have then enhanced The Conversation through every single touch point – be it events, stockists, the website, PR, or the product and its packaging.[7]

---

[7] If you'd like to hear more about Sue's business, you can hear my interview with her at eCommerceMasterPlan.com/Podcast.

What is "The Conversation"?

The Conversation is a continuous interaction between the business and the customer. Encompassing every single interaction a business has with a customer, this could include:

- An email they receive from your business.
- Someone talking about your business on a forum.
- An advert they see.
- Someone raving about one of your products on a TV show.
- Your business appearing in search engine results.
- Your business appearing on their Facebook newsfeed or in a search.
- One of their friends talking about using your business.
- Each time they visit your website or physical store.

The Conversation with you will be different for every customer. Different interaction points, a different mix of messages.

Many of the interaction points are very subtle, and the customer probably doesn't remember them all. We've all seen the results of putting "Where did you first hear about us?" in a survey – it's clear no one can remember!

The further the customer gets through the model, the more intimate The Conversation can become. They go from seeing adverts and PR, to receiving (possibly personalised) emails, and from receiving a parcel to being invited to pick some of the next season's flavours.

The more intimate The Conversation becomes, the more powerful it is, but also the greater the loss becomes if you screw up. As the intimacy of The Conversation builds, the customer is moving further right on the model. The further across the model the customer gets, the more they are worth to you and the more they expect of you – if you screw up at this point, you lose a valuable customer and it can be much harder to win them back.

This isn't a route-to-purchase model with a beginning and an end. The Conversation never ends. It continues throughout the lifetime of each customer's relationship with your business, encompassing every single interaction a customer has with your business, which means it's really important to make sure The Conversation is as good as it can be to maximise the CLV.

It's about what you say and what you do

Some of the most powerful elements of The Conversation are beyond your control.

These are the moments when someone else is talking about your business. They are powerful because people trust third parties talking about you more than they trust you telling them about you. The "someone else" could be another customer, or other influencers like TV, press, radio, bloggers, podcasters, and more. Anyone who is talking about your business and who the customer trusts.

Content Generated by Customers

Content generated by customers might be anything from reviews on your website, to a chat over coffee. It includes reviews on other websites, forums, and social media platforms, in print and in video.

According to a report from reviews software Bazaarvoice, customer generated content (CGC) influences at least 40% of all customers. This increases as income rises, with 87% of those earning over $150,000 being influenced by CGC, and increases with younger people, with 54% of 25 to 34-year-olds being influenced by CGC.[8]

Whilst you can put a reviews system on your website (and in 99% of cases you should), it won't stop customers from discussing you all over the place – and you don't want it to!

If customers understand your business, you want them to talk about you everywhere.

The role of a review system is to:

- Give you great feedback from your customers, which you can use to make your business better.
- Give you quotes and star ratings, which you can use in marketing to encourage purchases.
- Give your customers somewhere they can be part of your business, making them feel more involved.

All of this is great for The Conversation, but it's not where you want CGC to stop.

To make sure the right message is being conveyed about your business everywhere, you need to make sure your business is consistent in everything it says and everything it does. Unless you create the right experience, your customers won't be able to talk accurately about your business.

---

[8] "The Conversation Index Volume 9", Bazaarvoice, 2015.

How likely customers are to use each resource for pre-purchase research

Commercial Websites 90%

Price comparison sites, shopping guides........... 85%

Customer feedback sites........................ 74%

Ask close relatives for their opinion 74%

Ask shop attendants for their advice............... 56%

Media sites, online magazines.................... 42%

Paper magazines................................ 41%

On social media 38%

On blogs 36%

Customer services for commercial websites 29%

As you can see from this 2015 UK research by eDigital, customers are using all kind of information sources to do their pre-purchase research. And the great majority of these you have NO control over.[9]

Content Generated by Other Influencers

Often these are the most important interactions, and the ones that have the greatest ability to create or destroy the customers trust in your business. That's because the customer in question probably already has more trust in the TV show, radio host, podcast host, forum contributor, or in their friend than they do in your business. So if the person they're listening to is raving about you, some of the trust the customer has in the person speaking will be passed over to your business. The reverse is also true – if that person is criticising your business then it can massively erode a customer's trust in you.

---

[9] "The UK Customer Service & Support Market", eDigital Research and iAdvize, September 2015.

And sometimes this could be discussions about a product that's similar to yours, but not the one you sell. The Discovery Store (thediscoverystore.co.uk) in the UK had just this problem for Christmas 2015. They had predicted the hoverboard would be one of their best sellers despite its £399 price point. However in the run up to Christmas there was endless press coverage about the danger of these catching fire, horrible accidents and injuries, and their banning from several public spaces. Lots of misinformation and customer anguish meant hoverboard questions were their top customer service issue over the holiday, and sales were considerably lower than predicted.

Despite their stock having been tested by customs and passed without any issues, they had to reduce the price to £299 to clear it all. You can't avoid issues like that one, but you can go a long way to making sure interactions that are actually about your business get the right message across.

Whilst you don't have control over what the person on the TV is saying, if you're doing the best you can at everything within your control then it becomes much more likely that they'll be saying the right things, and if they get it wrong your customers will defend you.

How Your Customers Feel

You may have read the above and thought, "No customer will ever remember my delivery Ts & Cs!". You're probably right – they might not remember the details, but they will remember the emotions they feel when they deal with you.

It's the job of The Conversation to make sure interactions are effective, show that it's easy to do business with you, and most importantly create a feeling of engagement and positive emotion when customers deal with your business.

As Maya Angelou, American author, poet and civil rights activist, said:

> *"I've learned that people will forget what you said, people will forget what you did, but people will never forget how you made them feel."*

So what emotion do you want your customers to feel? Excited? Safe? Happy? Expectant? Relaxed?

Why do you need to think about "The Conversation"?

Whether you think about The Conversation customers are having with your business or not, it's happening.

The role of The Conversation is to generate the next step of getting a customer to sign up or to buy.

Conversation ➡ Conversion

The better The Conversation is, the more likely customers are to convert and the faster they will reach a point where they want to buy. The Conversation is all about building a trustworthy relationship between your business and the customer. The more you trust someone, the more likely to you are to buy from them.

When I'm in London, I stay in a hotel on Praed Street (between Paddington and Edgware Road). One of the great things about Praed Street is that you can get twenty different types of food or takeaway, all within a ten-minute walk. When it's been a long day and I just want to eat and chill out, I'll grab myself a KFC. Not the most glamourous choice but an easy go-to because it's a known quantity for me. I've been eating (very occasionally!) at KFC since 2000, and I still order the exact same meal now as I did then, and as far as I can remember it still tastes just as good. Last year I was having a waver and considering trying to be a bit more conscious of the food I put in my body – but then along came a three-episode documentary on the BBC, which went behind the scenes of KFC. The programme was fascinating, leaving me thinking what a great business it is and that there's nothing very wrong with the food. KFC haven't done a lot of marketing to keep my business coming, but they have been consistent, which is why about once a month I walk past two other fried chicken takeaways to get my 'I-need-a-chilled-evening' dinner of choice.

Zappos, a business owned by Amazon with a turnover of more than $2bn, are the biggest and best example in the world of the power of The Conversation. Their CEO Tony Hsieh said, "We take most of the money that we could have spent on paid advertising and instead put it back into the customer experience. Then we let the customers be our marketing".[10]

I'm not suggesting you immediately turn off all your paid marketing, but as you improve The Conversation conversions will come in more quickly and conversion rates will go up. All of that should improve your return on marketing investment, maybe to the point where you can follow in Tony Hsieh's footsteps. So it's important that as you improve your Customer MasterPlan, you also (as I know you all already do!) evaluate your marketing performance and spending plans on a regular basis – say every six to twelve months.

How do you improve The Conversation's ability to build trust?

The Conversation is clearly very important to the growth and future stability of a business, so you really should be thinking about how to improve it. But what does improving it mean?

---

10   If you haven't yet read *Delivering Happiness* by Tony Hsieh – read it. (But not until you've finished my book!!)

You need to increase the trust that it builds. There are a few key ways to increase trust within The Conversation.

Delivering on promises

You need to make sure that your business is doing what it says it will, and that you're keeping things up to date and accurate. If it's January and your website still says "Happy Christmas", that's not a good thing.

Being consistent

The simple side of consistency is the frequency of your messaging and its placement. This could include sending an email every week, your catalogue always arriving in September, featuring in The Times "Top 100 Gifts for Women" spread every year, or having a stall at the local Cancer charity event each year. If you've ever wondered why a failing business conference seems to take so long to die off, it's usually because enough of the exhibitors are too worried to cancel – concerned that if they're not at the show, potential and existing customers will think they're no longer in business or are in trouble.

It also means a consistent brand look and feel across your materials, so each interaction feels like it came from the same place. This literally means same colour palette, fonts, design style, and logos.

Providing the information customers want or expect from you

A few standard pieces of content are expected to appear on every site: the "About Us" page, contact details, and product information.

Depending on the business, there is other information that will be important to the customers. Listen to the questions the customers ask and make that information available.

Eradicating inaccuracies

Inaccuracies quickly erode trust. An offer that doesn't exist on the website anymore, or the delivery page missing the pricing option for the product you want to buy, or out-of-stock products showing at the top of categories.

Anything that wastes the customer's time or gives them misinformation is bad – so get it fixed! The sort of information you need to provide is different at each Stage of The Customer MasterPlan, and I'll discuss it all in the following chapters.

Keeping The Conversation consistent

It's clear that to build an effective Conversation, the message has to be the same through every interaction. That means everyone in your team, from full-time staff to your suppliers and more, needs to understand what that means. You can't sign off every last action. Consistency is much easier to create and monitor in small businesses than in large businesses, and a great way to embed it is with an Editorial Mission Statement. Your business mission also has a part to play, but so much has been written about business missions that I'm not going to cover them here.

The Editorial Mission Statement

Huge swathes of The Conversation happen in the content on your website and in your marketing – the words, images, audio, and video you're putting out there.

It's critical that they all help make The Conversation more powerful and elicit that emotion you want to create in your customers.

To tie all your content together, it's a good idea to have an Editorial Mission Statement.

This is usually completely different from a business mission. The Editorial Mission Statement explains what content you believe is the right content for your audience (the customers you want to be experiencing The Conversation).

It should include three things:

- Who your core audience is – the type of customer you want to be consuming your content and buying your products.
- The deliverables – the sort of information you're going to be providing them, or (if it's easier to think of it this way) what the value is within your content.
- What the audience gets from that content – what's in it for them?

That might sound a little complex, but it really isn't. Here are some examples of great Editorial Mission Statements:

- **Inc.com**
  Welcome to Inc.com, the place where entrepreneurs and business owners can find useful information, advice, insights, resources and inspiration for running and growing their businesses.

- **Homemadesimple.com**
  Whether it's a delicious recipe, an inspiring décor idea or a refreshing approach to organizing, we strive to help [Moms] create a home that's truly your own. Everything we do here is designed to empower and inspire you to make your home even better, and most importantly, a place you love to be.

- **Sports Illustrated**
  [Sports Illustrated] covers the people, passions and issues of numerous sports with the journalistic integrity that has made it the conscience of all sport. It is surprising, engaging and informative, and always with a point of view that puts its readers "in the game".

I haven't managed to find any examples from retailers, but I've taken the liberty of inventing some based on what I know about certain businesses...

- **ASOS**
  Where 20-somethings come to find out what's happening in affordable fashion, engage with their peers, and keep their look up to date.

- **Beardbrand**
  Beardbrand is an American business on a mission, their Vision is "to change the way society views beardsmen," shifting the perception of people with facial hair away from the common negative stereotypes, and "to foster style for the urban beardsman." I think their Editorial Mission would be where the urban beardsman comes to find out how to look after his beard, and take inspiration from how other men with facial hair are being viewed by society.

- **The Discovery Store**
  Where house-proud 30-somethings come to discover the next great home accessory to make their lives easier and more fun, whilst impressing their friends with their fashion-forward décor.

It's a pretty simple thing, but a really useful tool to make sure The Conversation is consistent across all your content.

Here's ours at eCommerce MasterPlan:

- **eCommerce MasterPlan**
  Where the small-to-medium online retailer can find inspiration, guidance and enlightenment specifically tailored to their needs, all designed to help them make the right decisions in their business – either to stick with the plan they already have, or how to change, tweak and optimise it. Ultimately helping you to build your business more easily.

The Customer Voice word cloud

As well as keeping everything that the business creates consistent with the Editorial Mission Statement, a Customer Voice word cloud can be a really handy way to understand what your customers want to hear about.

A word cloud is a visual representation of the relative importance of different words within a provided set of text. The bigger the word, the more often it appears in the text.

If you can get customers to answer the question "Why do you love {insert your product category here}?", then you can group all those answers together to create a word cloud of what's important to your customers when they think of your product.

For example:

- For Beardbrand, the question could be "What do you love most about your beard?" or "Why do you have a beard?".
- For ASOS, it could be "My clothes make me feel....".
- For The Discovery Store, "I want my home to be...".

There are several online tools you can use to create them; just give "word cloud" a Google search. Here are my two top tips to make them more useful:

1. Some word cloud tools pay attention to capitals, so you'll get "Home" and "home" separately in the results. Before uploading your text, do a "find and replace" in MS Word to change all the capital letters to lower case, e.g. "find A and replace with a".

2. When you first create the word cloud, if you get a really big word that's really obvious remove it from the text and re-create the word cloud. For example, if Beardbrand used the question above they'd probably get "beard" and "beards" as the biggest words – this doesn't help! So I would remove those words from the text and re-do the word cloud creation. It's going to be a LOT more useful!

Once the word cloud exists, it gives you a clear and simple guide to what your customers are interested in and what they want to hear from you about. The word cloud image should be distributed to everyone who interacts with or creates things that interact with customers. It can then be used to influence every piece of content that's created. It also becomes a great resource for working out what subjects to focus the marketing calendar on.

The Conversation is an essential part of The Customer MasterPlan

Whilst The Conversation is a critical part of getting customers to buy from you, it's very hard to measure! Neither you nor your customer would be able to outline all the moments of The Conversation.

So whilst you can't control every single message that gets out there, you can work out:

- What the message should be (your Editorial Mission Statement).
- The key touch points for your customers, and therefore where you need to make The Conversation the strongest (think back to the start of this chapter and Sue's wool bands).
- How to be consistent in thought and deed.

The Conversation is not just about what you say, it's also about what your business does – and those two should match up.

Eventually, every part of each customer's experience with your business will be part of The Conversation you've designed. It's going to take a while to get there.

In each of the following chapters, I'll provide you with examples of how others have used The Conversation at that Stage, and what the most important steps are to building your Conversation and performance in that Stage.

As you read through the Stages, you'll see how The Conversation builds from Stage 1 through to Stage 5 – so everything you improve in The Conversation for Stage 1 will improve performance in the Stages thereafter. If you hit a brick wall in improving one of your Stages, take a look at The Conversation ideas in the previous Stage. That might be where you can make the greatest impact.

Never forget, The Conversation is about how your business makes the customer FEEL.

So that's enough of the enlightenment – it's time to delve into the practicalities of how to get more customers from one side of the model to the other!

4 Stage 1: Attracting the Right Visitors

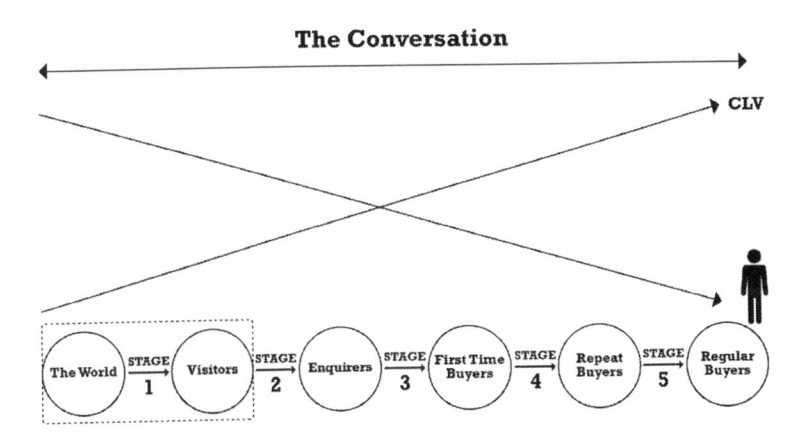

The Conversation

CLV

The World →STAGE 1→ Visitors →STAGE 2→ Enquirers →STAGE 3→ First Time Buyers →STAGE 4→ Repeat Buyers →STAGE 5→ Regular Buyers

STAGE 1 is where everything starts for your business. It's all about making people aware that your business exists and encouraging them to visit your website. Usually, it's a mixture of awareness-building PR and content marketing, as well as more direct call to action marketing like Google Adwords and direct mail.

Customer Persuasion | 55

Stage 1 is a very important part of The Customer MasterPlan.

- It's the first step on a customer's journey with your business.
- It's a gateway step – a customer can't visit your site, enquire, or buy without first being made aware your business exists.
- It's where The Conversation starts.
- It's where you are talking to and influencing the largest number of people, so it's the only time in this process that you get to choose who you're talking to. Throughout the rest of The Customer MasterPlan, you're only talking to those who've been through a previous step.
- It's where each customer you interact with is worth the least to you, so any resources spent must be spent wisely to make sure you're getting the impact you need.

It's the Stage that offers both the most potential and the greatest risk.

It's also the Stage where customers can lurk unseen for a long time, still experiencing The Conversation. It may be years of unrecorded customer interactions before the unknown customer finally visits your site. This makes it pretty much impossible to quantify or fully understand the impact of marketing and other actions on this Stage (another reason why a consistent Conversation is so important).

For many people reading this, it's probably the Stage you spend the most time thinking about and working on, probably more time than is spent on all the other Stages put together, but (as you'll discover reading this book) it's probably not the one you should be prioritising.

Miso Tasty (misotasty.com) is the UK's first dedicated miso brand. They're breaking new ground, with a new type of ingredient for the UK consumer. Bonnie Chung knew that for her business to survive, it was essential to build awareness of both miso and her business fast. She wasn't going to be able to rely on Google Adwords and natural search traffic because this is a product no-one knew they wanted. It also wasn't possible to list-buy, as the customer profile wasn't yet known.

There are two key methods Miso Tasty used to achieve that awareness.

- **PR:** Using the great story behind the product, the quality of the product, and different ways to use it (lots of recipes!) to get coverage in key UK titles. They focused on those that their target markets were most likely to read: national papers, food & lifestyle magazines, and the occasional celebrity chef and food blogger.

- **Wholesaling:** Customers need to try the product, so get into the places where people try food products! Their soups were made available at high-end UK supermarkets, including Waitrose, Sainsbury's, and Ocado. They were also in key designer department stores, such as Selfridges and Harvey Nichols. Those of you in the US, think Barneys and Nordstrom. Plus, they're in Whole Foods Market in the UK, as well as several specialist food stores based in the health and gourmet side of things. No one goes into any of these locations looking for miso soup, but this strategy put Bonnie's products in front of customers who might be interested, in an environment where they're thinking about food. This directly impacts online sales and does a great job of building brand awareness. And all whilst making a profit!

This was all backed up with great content on the website, so that anyone searching for them would find them, and a strong social media presence.[11]

---

[11] If you'd like to hear more about how Bonnie's growing Miso Tasty, you can listen to her podcast interview at eCommerceMasterPlan.com/podcast.

What's the aim of Stage 1?

The aim of this Stage is to get customers to interact with your business by visiting your website or your physical store.

To do this, you need to identify who your business should be trying to attract, grab their attention, and get them interested in your business. They need to be interested enough to take the action to visit you.

Where does a social media follower fit in?

In Stage 1, you're trying to get someone to your website so that in Stage 2 you can get their email address. The reason you are focused on an email address is that the email address is owned by you and the customer; there's no 3rd party who can suddenly shut down your ability to communicate with your email list. This is unlike a Facebook "like" that could be taken from you or devalued by Facebook at any point. It's also possible that Facebook might remove your Page, or even the whole idea of Pages! Even a change in the newsfeed algorithm could have a negative impact. For these reasons, Facebook is unpredictable and your business should never solely rely on it to connect with your customers.

Gathering social media followers is always a good idea (if they're the type of customers you want to speak to of course!) but it's just a step on the pathway to getting them to your website, not a goal in itself.

It's possible – maybe even easy, although probably not free – to get 10,000 followers on social media, and it's not too hard to get 10,000 addresses onto your email list. The really hard part is getting 10,000 customers who are actively interested in your business onto your email list.

How does The Conversation fit into this Stage?

The Conversation starts in this Stage.

It's essential that everything you put out there in this Stage fits with your Editorial Mission – it has to be consistent and accurately reflect your business.

Whilst the aim of The Conversation at this Stage is to get them to the website, it should also be laying down the groundwork for encouraging them to sign up or buy, seeding that idea in their subconscious.

Conversationally this is the most challenging Stage because you are talking to customers who have not heard of you before, and there may be several conversational interactions before the customer takes action. So you have to work harder to achieve your aims.

Key messages at this point will include:

- We exist(!).
- We sell A, B, and C.
- X, Y, and Z are our values.
- We know lots about our subject.

(Please don't use ANY of those phrases in your marketing!)

It's all about big brand statements, statements that make the customer aware of your business and start to build their trust by showing your expertise.

What can my existing customers teach me about what I should be doing at this Stage?

A great way to improve your marketing is to listen to what your customers are loving about your brand and put that out there for more people to see.

So take a read of your customer testimonials. What do they rave about? Is it your shipping policies, your products, your customer service?

Including those messages when you're working to attract new customers to your business will both increase response rates and help bring in the right customers. If the new customers are attracted by the things that the existing customers love, you're bringing in customers who are going to love you too.

Research and preparation

You can't afford to market to the entire world. And to make it more complicated, there are hundreds of different ways to get customers to your website.

This is the Stage where you need to put the most effort into working out what you're going to do before you give it a go. That means you have to do some research.

I'm going to outline some different ways you can research both how you're going to target the right sort of people, and what marketing methods you could be using.

The effectiveness of each of these research methods will change from business to business, so start with those you think will fit best for you. If you get results that tell you something you can act on, then get on with the marketing and come back again later to explore another research method. If you don't learn anything you can use with your first research method, try another research method.

You can come back to the research list again in the future when you are ready to find more customer attraction methods.

Things to remember before you start on the research and marketing:

- You don't want to attract everyone to your business. The word "potential" is critical – you're looking for people with the potential to be great customers, not just anyone.

- To attract unknown potential customers effectively, you're going to need to use a mix of marketing methods. Just one is unlikely to work.

- These marketing methods are NOT to bring back existing customers, or existing Enquirers – they are purely to attract the unknown potential customer.

Research Method 1: Using your existing data

There is a wealth of information in data you already have at your fingertips, both to identify potential marketing methods and target customers.

If you already have some great customers (people who have bought from you and were not disappointed) then it would make sense to work on attracting people who are like them to your business.

- Mine your existing data. Take the buyers' details and look at where in the world they are. Think about focusing your marketing in those areas. This might mean you're targeting just one country or area inside a country.

- Profile your data – have your files run against a demographics / psychographics file.

  I don't recommend this as a starting point as it doesn't give you practical actions, just a lot of very interesting information about your customers.

- Look at the geo/demo/psycho-graphics of your social media followers.

  Obviously this doesn't only represent your buyers, but assuming you haven't forced the growth of your followers the stats should be representative.

These existing data sources will help you find out more about your customers:

Twitter Analytics

Log in to your Twitter account and navigate to the "Analytics" information. You'll find the following information about your followers:

- Gender mix
- Geographic data
- Interest areas
- TV Genres
- Device type (how they are accessing Twitter)

Gender

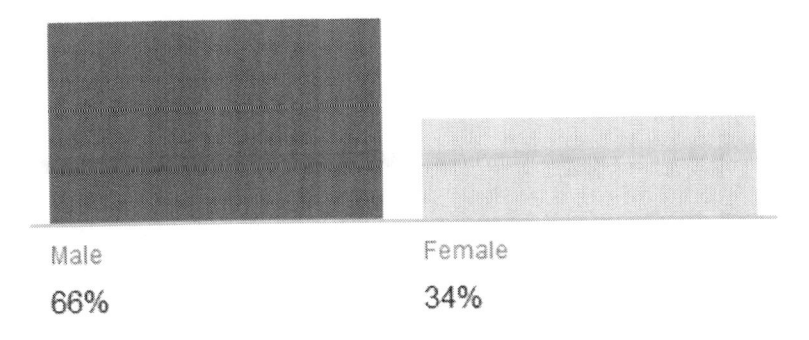

Male
66%

Female
34%

Country name	% of audience
United Kingdom	62%
United States	17%

State or region	% of audience
England, GB	59%
Greater London, GB	15%
South East England, GB	14%
South West England, GB	12%
East England, GB	4%

Interest name	% of audience
Technology	75%
Entrepreneurship	73%
Marketing	73%
Business and finance	72%
Tech news	69%
Business news and general info	65%
Startups	59%
Leadership	54%
Business and news	53%
SEO	47%

TV Genres

Genre name	% of audience
Sports	56%
Drama	53%
Reality	40%
Documentary & Special Interest	35%
Comedy	35%
Movies	32%
Talk	27%
Other	26%
Sci-fi	23%
News	19%

Device type	% of audience
iOS devices	44%
Android devices	24%
Blackberry phones and tablets	< 1%
Mobile web on other devices	1%
Desktop and laptop computers	82%

By looking at the results for our Twitter account, my business can learn:

- It's not worth gender targeting our marketing as our product is gender neutral and over 30% of our audience are women. So we won't be running men-only ads!

- For PR, adverts, and ad targeting we should focus on appearing in technology and business media outlets.

- Not only should we focus our ad spend on the UK, we should focus on London and the south.

- The TV genres information doesn't tell us much that we can use, so I'm going to ignore that (not all research will be useful for everyone).

- The majority of my followers are using desktop rather than mobile, so to create advertising and marketing specifically targeting mobile users would be a waste of time and effort.

Facebook Page Insights

These are freely available to any Facebook Page user.[12] Just log in to your Page and navigate to the "Insights" area to find out more information about your Page fans and those who see your posts, including:

- Gender and age mix
- Geographic location (country and city)
- Languages

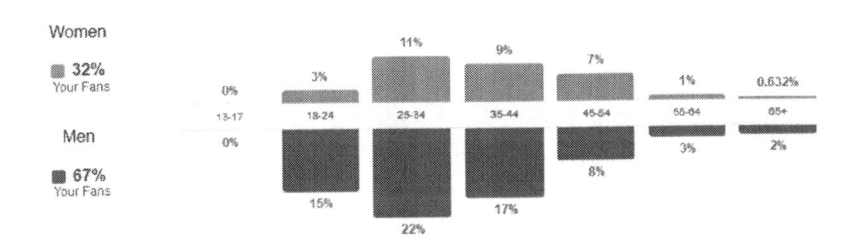

Women
■ 32% Your Fans

	13-17	18-24	25-34	35-44	45-54	55-64	65+
Women	0%	3%	11%	9%	7%	1%	0.632%
Men	0%	15%	22%	17%	8%	3%	2%

Men
■ 67% Your Fans

---

[12] We don't prioritise our Facebook Page, it just kinda ticks over for us – but that doesn't mean the analytics aren't going to be helpful for identifying potential customers.

Country	Your Fans	City	Your Fans	Language	Your Fans
United Kingdom	379	London, England	73	English (US)	530
India	348	New Delhi, Delhi	24	English (UK)	399
United States of America	77	Dublin, Dublin	23	Hindi	5
Ireland	47	Calcutta, West Bengal	19	English (India)	4
Australia	29	Mumbai, Maharashtra	11	Romanian	2
New Zealand	27	Hyderabad, Telangana	11	Russian	1

Looking at the eCommerce MasterPlan Facebook Page, I can see:

- A very similar gender split to Twitter – so we'll continue to ignore gender segmenting.

- Our most popular age range is 25 to 34, but we have good coverage from 18 up to 54. So we should avoid focusing on those over 55 and under 18. Due to the fact we're targeting people in business, we should probably not pay to advertise to under 22s.

- Our reach is greatest in the UK, yet we have quite a lot of Indians – that's due to some get-likes advertising we did in 2015. It was an interesting test, but ultimately we should have left India out of the ads (great Facebook Ad engagement, terrible conversions). So again, the lesson here is to only pay for traffic from the UK for now.

Pinterest Analytics

These are available if you've authenticated your Pinterest business account.

Just log in and go the "Analytics" area to see who's interacting with your account and, if you've authenticated your website, what people are pinning from your website. This includes:

- Geographic location (country and city – "metro")
- Interests
- Brands (other businesses your audience engages with)

Country	Audience
United Kingdom	967
United States	379
Canada	58
Australia	34
France	31

Metro	Audience
Washington, DC (Hagrstwn)	22
New York	21
San Francisco-Oak-San Jose	20
Los Angeles	16
Chicago	16

Interests: What your audience is into

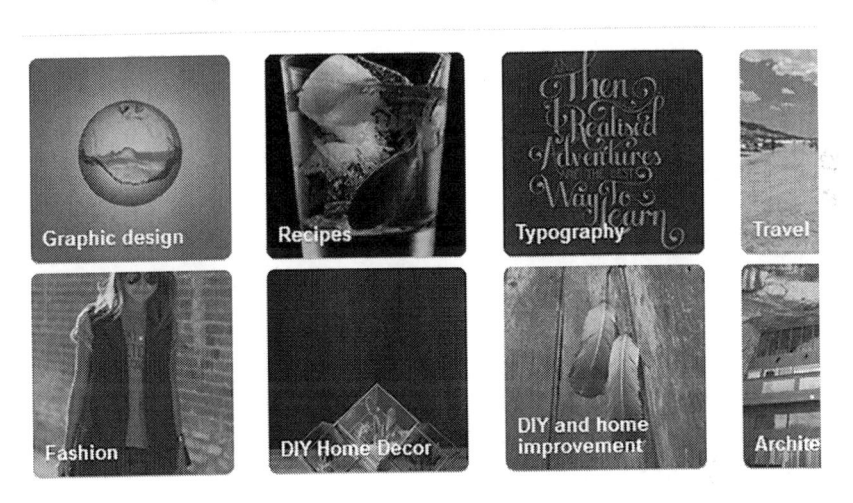

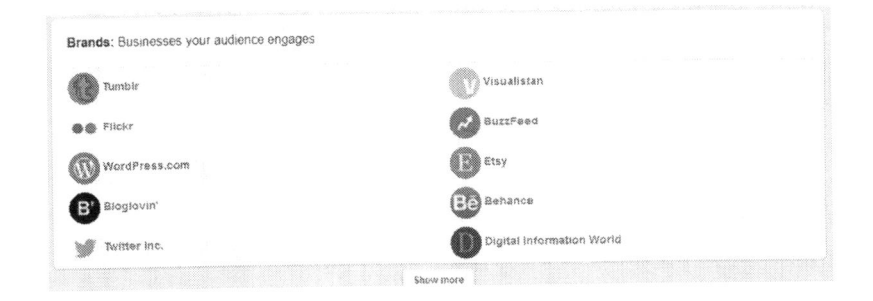

- Graphic design
- Recipes
- Typography
- Travel
- Fashion
- DIY Home Decor
- DIY and home improvement
- Archite[cture]

Brands: Businesses your audience engages

- Tumblr
- Flickr
- WordPress.com
- Bloglovin'
- Twitter Inc.
- Visualistan
- BuzzFeed
- Etsy
- Behance
- Digital Information World

Show more

You can also get gender information from Pinterest, but because Pinterest users are more likely to be women this is going to give a biased answer. So I don't recommend reading too much into it.

Based on the eCommerce MasterPlan Pinterest board:

- The country mix continues to show the same story, telling us to start off focused on the UK then go for the USA, Canada, and Australia.

- Interests – there are a few curveballs in here (travel, art, DIY, Star Wars, and recipes!). That's partly because we used to have a policy of putting a few personal bits and pieces up there, so there was a recipes board at one point, but also because that's primarily what Pinterest is about. Read this one with a bit of care. This isn't giving us anything I couldn't have taken from the other social channels' data.

- Brands – this can throw up some interesting information, but I'm not able to learn a lot from it. Whilst Buzzfeed is very popular with our followers, it's not a site I'm going to prioritise getting mentioned on. Saying that, I might take a look at "Digital Information World".

Social media channels are increasingly making this sort of information available. If there's another one you like to use, go and see what they'll tell you.

As well as looking at the social media data, you should take a look at your Google Analytics account. (If you don't yet have Google Analytics up and running for your website – stop reading and get it done! It doesn't take a lot of time, and it will provide endlessly useful information.)

Google Analytics
In the "Audience" section on Google Analytics, you can find out lots about the Visitors to your website. I would value the stats about people from your website more than those about people on your social media channels. Google Analytics includes:

- Gender information

- Age mix
- Geographic (country, region or state, city)

For every single one of these reports, you can choose to see a table of results in the normal Google Analytics ABC format (Acquisition, Behaviour and Conversions, as illustrated in the Gender graphic below). This is really useful as you can see the value of that traffic. In this Stage, you're looking for interested Visitors (not necessarily the converters) so you should look at pages per session and session duration, as well as the conversion rate.

	Acquisition			Behavior			Conversions
Gender	Sessions	% New Sessions	New Users	Bounce Rate	Pages / Session	Avg. Session Duration	Goal Conversion Rate
	1,134 % of Total 69.83% (1,624)	57.76% Avg for View 61.45% (-6.01%)	655 % of Total 85.63% (998)	70.19% Avg for View 71.82% (-2.40%)	1.71 Avg for View 1.87 (-2.28%)	00:02:06 Avg for View 00:01:52 (12.40%)	4.23% Avg for View 4.31% (-1.80%)
1. male	659 (58.11%)	57.66%	380 (58.02%)	70.86%	1.58	00:01:25	4.86%
2. female	475 (41.89%)	57.89%	275 (41.98%)	69.26%	1.88	00:03:02	3.37%

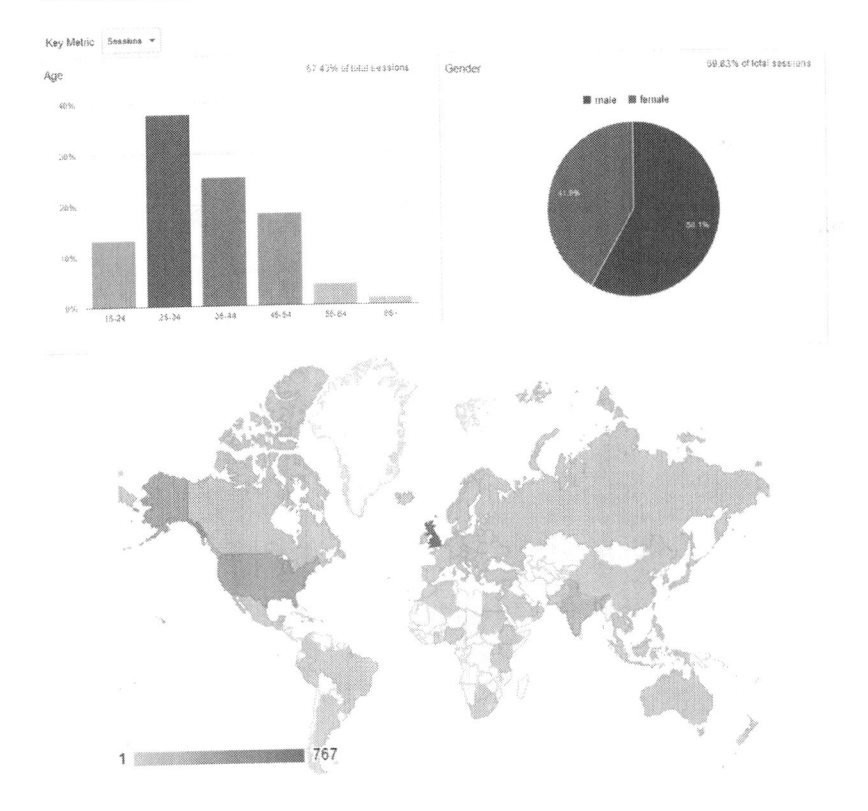

Looking at the eCommerceMasterPlan.com analytics:

- Whilst the age profile of Visitors to our site peaks at 25 to 35, it still shows that 25-55 is where we should be putting our effort.
- Gender wise, we see the same scenario.
- Geographic gives a nice map, and we can dive in to see our customers in each country, state, region, etc., too. Again, a similar picture to social media, so we should focus any paid advertising on the UK.

Once you've mined all these resources that are freely at your disposal, write a summary of who in the world you feel you should be targeting with your attraction marketing. At a minimum, this should include:

- Geographic criteria (countries, cities, regions).
- Demographic criteria (age, gender).
- Interests data.

You may have subcategories within this, e.g. if we're paying for the advertising then we want to restrict it to X criteria, but if it's a piece of PR or content marketing we're very happy for it to become broader. For PR at eCommerce MasterPlan, I'm happy to write articles for websites and magazines anywhere in the world, but my advertising spend should be focused on the UK.

You may also have picked up some idea of what marketing methods you might want to use, as well as places to market in. Make a note of those as well.

Research Method 2: Using your existing data to understand what marketing methods you should use

Planning your marketing for Stage 1 is not about ripping up everything you're already doing and starting again, it's about identifying what you should keep doing to attract unknown potential customers and building on that.

Just like you have a lot of existing information about who your customers are to help you chose how to target unknown potential customers, you also have a lot of existing information about traffic methods that work well for you.

So, you need to look at what marketing you're doing and how it's working for you.

For an example, here is the Google Analytics Source/Medium report for eCommerceMasterPlan.com. You can find this report under Behaviour, detailing the "Source" of the traffic (such as a search engine, social media, or another website) and the "Medium" (what sort of link it was, like a pay-per-click or in an email). For now, you want to look PURELY at the New Users segment:

Source / Medium	Sessions	% New Sessions	New Users	Bounce Rate	Pages / Session	Avg. Session Duration	Goal Conversion Rate
New Users	11,469 % of Total 72.99% (15,714)	100.00% Avg for View 72.99% (37.01%)	11,469 % of Total 100.00% (11,469)	77.40% Avg for View 72.89% (6.17%)	1.50 Avg for View 1.57 (-10.13%)	00:01:00 Avg for View 00:01:31 (-33.86%)	1.46% Avg for View 3.76% (-61.05%)
1. google / organic	4,738 (41.31%)	100.00%	4,738 (41.31%)	78.39%	1.43	00:01:01	1.39%
2. (direct) / (none)	2,165 (18.88%)	100.00%	2,165 (18.88%)	74.36%	1.61	00:01:15	1.57%
3. google / cpc	1,079 (9.41%)	100.00%	1,079 (9.41%)	89.25%	1.10	00:00:07	0.00%
4. twitter / post	444 (3.87%)	100.00%	444 (3.87%)	81.08%	1.29	00:01:00	0.68%
5. t.co / referral	407 (3.55%)	100.00%	407 (3.55%)	86.00%	1.32	00:00:36	0.49%
6. chloethomas.com / referral	359 (3.13%)	100.00%	359 (3.13%)	53.48%	2.18	00:01:31	4.74%
7. facebook / post	252 (2.20%)	100.00%	252 (2.20%)	95.63%	1.07	00:00:05	0.00%
8. infusionsoft / email	219 (1.91%)	100.00%	219 (1.91%)	71.69%	1.58	00:01:22	2.74%
9. m.facebook.com / referral	209 (1.82%)	100.00%	209 (1.82%)	89.95%	1.10	00:00:23	0.00%
10. facebook / cpc	146 (1.27%)	100.00%	146 (1.27%)	94.52%	1.08	00:00:07	0.00%

(If you're getting low numbers – say less than 5,000 sessions in total – expand the data range until you do have 5,000 plus. It will make the results more reliable.)

From this, my business can learn:

- **Facebook Ads:** At number 10, very low response and poor engagement.
- **Google Ads:** Number 3. Drives a lot more volume than Facebook ads but equally poor engagement

If you get less-than-impressive ad results like these, it's time to leave Google Analytics and login to your advertising platforms to see what was actually going on.

Was it a test-heavy time when you were doing a lot of experimenting? Were there some bits that worked and you should keep it in the mix? Is there room for improvement? Or were you doing everything you could, and doing it right? If that's the case and the results are like the above – look at how an expert might be able to help and try outsourcing, or don't do the advertising!

- **Twitter:** At both 4 and 5 (t.co is also Twitter), it's bringing in lots of engaged people. We should keep working on Twitter, and maybe test some Twitter ads too.
- **ChloeThomas.com:** Referrals from my website are very strong, so maybe we need to put some work into that site? We do tend to ignore it!
- **Direct Emails:** These are doing well at number 8, but we have to ignore them at this Stage, as we can't send an email to an unknown potential customer!
- **Organic and Direct:** These are at the top of the list, but don't give us anything actionable to get those unknown potential customers. We'll leave these at this Stage.

If you're running marketing that doesn't track into Google Analytics, you should review those results too. These might be mailing lists, insert campaigns, PR, or other methods.

Make sure you create a summary of all you've learnt from this. What you've discovered, what ideas it's sparked, what you want to test next.

Research Method 3: Ask your customers!

There are lots of free tools you can use for this. Google Docs? Survey Monkey? Have a search around and find one that suits you.

Make sure to ask:

- Their age.
- What newspapers and magazines they buy, read, or download.
- What other shops they buy from.
- What social media they use.

Those questions are structured to provide data that will enable practical targeting of unknown potential customers. You could put an ad in the media source the majority of them read, form a partnership with one of the other shops they buy from, or advertise on the most popular social media channel.[13]

Avoid open text responses if at all possible because they are very hard to analyse. I highly recommend you brainstorm the opinions of your staff to create a list of answers for each question and style the response as a tick list including an "other"

---

13 And if you're thinking you could add in the word cloud questions from the last chapter – great idea!

option. This will make the data more useful, and much, much easier to analyse.

There's then lots of ways to get responses.

- Email it to your buyers or your full list.
- Put a prepaid postcard version into your parcels.
- Put a link to it on your order confirmation page.
- Push it on your Facebook Page.

You'll probably want to re-run this every year.

The most important thing is to remember to analyse the results!

Research Method 4: Competitor analysis

So far, I've focused on looking at yourself and your own business.

Wouldn't it make choosing marketing methods to use so much easier if you knew what your competitors were having success with? Well, you can do that! And it's not as difficult as you might think.

The Watching Method

First, you need to identify any businesses who are selling similar products to and/or targeting the same customers as you.

Then subscribe to everything they've got!

- Sign up to emails or newsletters.
- Buy something from them.
- Follow them on each of their social media profiles.
- Add an RSS feed of their blog to a feedly account.

- Set up Google Alerts of their brand name so you can see where they appear online.

If they try something once and don't do it again, you can assume it didn't work. If they try something and keep doing it, you can assume it worked really well!

The Watching Method is something you could be doing all the time. As there are probably only a handful of companies to watch, it shouldn't be too time consuming.

Admittedly not all of what you will pick up is relevant to Stage 1, but you might as well set up all of the following in one go!

Google Analytics Benchmarking Facilities

These have come on leaps and bounds in recent years. Now you can see how you fare against other businesses in your category (you can drill it right down to retail, and in my case down to "eCommerce Services"), your region, and with similar traffic volumes to you.

Stats for comparison includes the Acquisition and Behaviour of the Google dashboard, so you can see traffic volumes and engagement on the website, but not conversion.

You can analyse it in terms of the different devices traffic is coming through on, the geographic locations they're getting traffic from, and (most importantly for this piece of research) on the channels.

76 | Customer Persuasion

Default Channel Grouping	Sessions	% New Sessions	New Users	Pages / Session	Avg. Session Duration	Bounce Rate
	138.82% ↑	14.72% ↓	103.67% ↑	30.26% ↓	9.99% ↑	13.47% ↓
	1,634 vs 685	61.45% vs 72.06%	995 vs 490	1.87 vs 2.29	00:01.52 vs 00:02.04	71.82% vs 63.32%
1. Organic Search	107.53% ↑	13.66% ↑	135.89% ↑	41.56% ↓	-51.12% ↓	34.87% ↑
	609 vs 292	84.91% vs 74.78%	502 vs 240	1.46 vs 2.51	00:01.09 vs 00:02:03	76.81% vs 56.43%
2. Direct	17.48% ↑	-17.86% ↓	-3.52% ↓	-43.33% ↓	-24.16% ↓	24.29% ↑
	336 vs 286	57.14% vs 69.56%	192 vs 199	1.46 vs 2.57	00:01:44 vs 00:02:17	78.49% vs 61.14%
3. Referral	16.73% ↑	-60.46% ↓	-53.65% ↓	-11.18% ↓	5.32% ↑	-17.66% ↓
	314 vs 269	28.98% vs 72.49%	90 vs 196	1.29 vs 3.12	00:02.09 vs 00:02.04	59.24% vs 72.12%
4. Social	-21.39% ↓	-34.98% ↓	-48.89% ↓	6.39% ↑	202.58% ↑	-3.53% ↓
	147 vs 187	46.94% vs 72.19%	68 vs 135	2.54 vs 2.39	00:06:40 vs 00:01:55	41.50% vs 64.17%
5. Email	-51.30% ↓	-21.37% ↓	-61.70% ↓	-48.60% ↓	-31.04% ↓	33.80% ↑
	94 vs 193	38.30% vs 48.70%	30 vs 94	1.90 vs 3.70	00:02.00 vs 00:03:05	61.70% vs 46.11%
6. (Other)	-77.37% ↓	-15.03% ↓	-80.77% ↓	-30.00% ↓	-32.73% ↓	11.33% ↑
	43 vs 190	55.14% vs 65.42%	25 vs 130	1.40 vs 2.10	00:01:18 vs 00:01:52	74.42% vs 66.84%
7. Paid Search	-99.72% ↓	22.79% ↑	-99.66% ↓	-50.48% ↓	-100.00% ↓	50.42% ↑
	1 vs 361	100.00% vs 81.44%	1 vs 294	1.00 vs 2.02	00:00:00 vs 00:01:30	100.00% vs 66.48%
8. Display	-100.00% ↓	-100.00% ↓	-100.00% ↓	-100.00% ↓	-100.00% ↓	-100.00% ↓
	0 vs 612	0.00% vs 79.90%	0 vs 489	0.00 vs 1.34	00:00:00 vs 00:00:20	0.00% vs 84.75%

This is our data from eCommerceMasterPlan.com. You can see:

- We perform MUCH better than the competition with our volume (sessions) of Organic Search traffic.
- We're doing better than average on Direct traffic and Referral (customers coming in via links on other websites).
- But we're way behind in pay-per-click traffic. There are big opportunities in Display and Paid Search. We're somewhat behind on Email and Social (media) too.

Moving on from the Sessions data to look at the headlines:

- We're getting more Sessions than the average in our benchmark.
- We're getting a better percentage of new users.
- But our engagement levels are behind our competition.

So I'm not just going to go for the marketing methods that others are getting more traffic from, I'm going to go for the marketing methods where others are getting more traffic AND getting much better engagement than I am.

That puts these marketing methods top of the list:

- Keep working the Organic Search.
- (I would say Direct but it's very hard to build this!)
- Our Referrals are great, so we should keep working on them.
- Social engagement is well ahead of the pack, but our traffic is below the pack. There's a BIG opportunity here.
- Email should clearly be giving us more, but I'm dealing with Stage 1 here and I still won't have the email address of the unknown potential customers.
- Seeing as everyone else is investing in traffic from Paid Search and getting reasonable engagement, it seems like we should give that another test.
- With Display, the engagement level is awful (the average time on site from this channel is just 20 seconds) so I'm going to ignore that one.

You can, of course, take this to next level by segmenting your Google Analytics data into just New Sessions, but you need a fair bit of data to make that meaningful, so I suggest you focus on all traffic for now.

This is fantastic data, but you'll have noticed that it's very generic – Paid Search and Social both cover a wide range of marketing methods. Whilst this is incredibly useful data, it's not yet giving me very practical guidance like "get on Twitter"!

Online Tools

There are several online tools to assist with competitor analysis. You can feed in the URL of one of your competitors and they'll give you lots of interesting stats. Usually, you'll get a few results for free and then have to pay for more. Basically a try-before-you-buy.

My current favourite is Similarweb.com, where you can get the top five results on a whole host of stats for free (so go and check it out!). The most useful for research into attracting unknown potential customers to your website are:

- The countries that they get their traffic from.
- The broad traffic mix – direct vs. referral, vs. search vs. social, and so on.
- Top referring sites – so the top sites their traffic comes from.
- Top organic keywords – what people are googling to find them.
- Their top paid keywords – if they're paying for traffic.
- Which social media engines are bringing them traffic.
- Any display advertising they are doing.
- Details about their audience, specifically their interests and other websites they've visited.

Social Media Audit

If you really want to dive into the social media of your competitors, I suggest you do a thorough survey rather than look at it piecemeal.

To understand where they're getting traction and putting in the effort, perform an audit of each of their social media channels. For each competitor, capture the stats which are available for free, e.g. on Twitter you can easily see how many followers they have, how many people they follow, and how many tweets they've put out there. On Facebook you can see how many Page likes they have, and a quick scroll down will give you an idea of how engaged their audience is. Try grading it out of 5.

If this feels like a very time consuming task, yes it is! If you prefer, you can outsource the bulk of it to a freelancer for $100 or less on Upwork.com or a similar freelancing site.

There is more research to be done in Stage 1 than in any other Stage, and the answers will impact decisions in every later Stage. It may take you some time, but it will be time well invested.

This research is critical for helping you to understand what marketing methods to invest your time, energy and money into, and to get a better idea of the types of messages you should be including as part of The Conversation.

Marketing actions to attract the right Visitors to your website

Once the research is complete, you should have a much better idea of the marketing methods you want to keep using and who you're going to be targeting your marketing at. Plus, some ideas of the messages you will be putting in front of them, and some ideas of new marketing to test out.

In this Stage, you usually need to be doing a range of marketing methods because there may need to be several interactions before you get the customer to your website.

You will be putting in an awful lot of marketing effort (time and money) to get a result, having to cover a few different bases, and do a lot of testing and measuring to get this right.

The marketing that works in Stage 1 can be split into three categories, broadly defined by the size of the audience and likelihood of creating a Visitor.

These three categories are a little bit like concentric circles getting ever closer to your website.

Shine a Light
The outer circle is marketing that shines a light on your business to make people aware you exist. It's the broadest targeting and least likely to get a Visitor directly to your site, but you will be hitting the largest volume of people.

Target Customer
The middle circle is marketing you put in places where it's highly likely to be seen by people who are your target customer. This

is putting your business in front of people who are like your customers – a smaller group of people to target – and is much more likely to get them to the website.

Get Found

The smallest circle is marketing that guarantees someone will find you when they are looking for what you sell. This targets the smallest volume of people, but a very high proportion of those should be directed to your site.

These three categories work very well together. Think back to The Conversation – it might start with a customer seeing some of your Shine a Light marketing, and then the next thing they come across is you guesting on a product niche podcast (Target Customers marketing). Finally, when they're looking for a specific product you sell, your site appears in the shopping results on Google (Get Found marketing).

Some marketing methods fit into more than one of these categories because they can be targeted in different ways. PR can be both Shine a Light and Target Customers. If it's an article about you or one of your products in a national newspaper, that's Shine a Light. But if it were the same content in a niche publication, it would be Target Customers. Google Adwords can be used at all levels, Display advertising would be Shine a Light, Display advertising to a "similar to" audience would be Target Customer, and Google Shopping Campaigns are Get Found marketing.

You may want to be doing some marketing from each of the three categories, and the importance of each category varies from business to business. Some can succeed purely with Get Found marketing (Johnny Lomax of William May Jewellers does this using Google Shopping Campaigns), whereas others rely on a mixture.[14] Find the mixture that works for you, and if you get every category right your overall cost per conversion will decrease.

Category 1: Shine a Light marketing

This is as close as you're going to get to traditional, above-the-line activity. It's the least trackable and will reach the most people, but it needn't be the most expensive option. In fact, the majority of these items you can do for free, although they do tend to be quite time consuming.

It's all about making your business look great to as many people as possible, and doing that on platforms that have very large audiences that are not totally irrelevant to you.

- An article could be written about your business (or by you) in a global or national magazine, or newspaper.
- You might be writing guest blogs for websites.
- An article mentioning you could appear on a popular website, such as BuzzFeed or Huffington Post.
- You might be a guest on TV, or have your products featured on a TV or radio show.
- You could be a guest on a podcast.[15]

That can also include selling platforms such as key retailers or marketplaces — wholesaling your product in order to build brand awareness. This is one that not a lot of people talk about, but it can be hugely powerful tool to build your business.

---

[14] You can hear my interview with Jonny, where we discuss this and more, at eCommerceMasterPlan.com/podcast.

[15] If you would like to be on the eCommerce MasterPlan Podcast, head over to the contact form on the website and we'll see what we can do for you. eCommerceMasterPlan.com/Contact.

The start of this chapter outlined how Miso Tasty have done this, and this has also been the launch route of choice for The TeaShed (the-teashed.co.uk), using placement in big supermarkets and department stores to build brand awareness and grow their online business.[16]

Category 2: Target Customer marketing

In this category the marketing gets a lot more targeted, but you may still be using the same methods. I write articles for a number of online news sites, pretty much the same type of content for each of the sites – some of this counts as "Shine a Light" marketing when it ends up on sites like MarketingDonut.com. But I write a lot more for eCommerce specific sites like eSeller.net or InternetRetailing.com.au, because that puts my content in front of my target customers as well as the business world.

The research covered earlier in the chapter will come in very handy here, especially:

- How old the customers are.
- Where they are.
- What they are interested in, in terms of topics and interests.
- What magazines and websites they go to for information about the thing you sell.

This knowledge will enable you to place online adverts in front of the right type of people, and identify niche websites and print publications that your customers are very likely to be consuming.

---

16 You can hear my interviews with both Bonnie from Miso Tasty and Jules from TeaShed at: eCommerceMasterPlan.com/podcast.

The key marketing methods you can use for this category are as follows.

Facebook Ads

This is one of the easiest marketing methods you can use to target people who fit your customer demographic.

Either select the audience based on the results of your research, or just use the CRM remarketing method to create a "lookalike" list. To do this, you upload a list of your customers to Facebook, where it will create a lookalike list of that list, a list of people who are similar to what Facebook knows about your customers.

However you decide to create your audience — just put ads in front of them about your business.

This method is very simple and very cost-effective.

Similarly straightforward versions of this are available on Google Adwords, Twitter, and other PPC marketplaces.

Digital Display Advertising

This is the same theory, but using much more complex software to put the adverts across a much wider range of websites, whilst targeting people who have a similar profile to those who've bought from your website.

Andrew Wilson of Allergy Best Buys has used this to quickly grow his business.[17]

---

[17] You can hear Andrew discussing this at: eCommerceMasterPlan.com/podcast.

Offline Direct Marketing

There are many ways to get your hands (legally!) on the postal address data of your target customer.

- Rent the data based on the demographic and psychographic profile you are targeting.
- Swap or rent data directly with other businesses that target the same customers as you do.
- Join a data co-operative – where lots of businesses in your sector pool customer information in order to enable each other to grow.

Media Outlets

In your investigations you should have identified some key publications, websites, podcasts, etc., that your target customer is likely to be paying attention to. Target them to try and get them to write a piece about you, feature a product, or even have you as a guest. It could just be a very simple advertising sponsorship deal to get your product consistently mentioned on their outlet.

Inserts & Off-The-Page

You can also pay to get in front of the customers who are consuming those media outlets you've identified. Online, this will simply be advertising on a website, but offline it can be really effective too.

There are two key ways to do it.

Off-the-page advertising is constructing adverts with very strong CTAs (usually to buy – so this may enable you to get some customers to jump straight from The World Level to the First

Time Buyer Level!) and placing them in the target print media. Done well, this can build a business on its own.[18]

The other option is to produce some inserts – a postcard or catalogue – that you pay to have delivered alongside the print publication.

Social Media

All your marketing activity will grow your following on social media. Assuming you've been putting out a consistent Conversation, your followers should be representative of your target customer.

The aim of Stage 1 is to get Visitors to your website. So putting great content out across your social media profiles should encourage the Target Customers that are your followers to become Visitors.

Category 3: Get Found marketing

One of the common problems for a smaller business is making sure that the people who want your product can find you when they want you. If someone is on the internet searching for your exact product, you need to make sure it's you that they find!

There are far fewer options to choose from for this category, so essentially this is all about keyword advertising and Google Shopping campaigns on AdWords. It's fairly straightforward.

This category also stretches to listing some of your products on marketplaces like Amazon and eBay, if that's where people are most commonly searching for what you do.

---

[18] This is how Martin Harvey has built Muck Munchers – find out all about that in my interview with him at: eCommerceMasterPlan.com/podcast.

How do you work out where to start?

There are many marketing actions you could take in Stage 1, so a little bit of work to find where to start will really pay off. You want to identify the marketing that has the greatest chance of success for you, and those that are clearly not a good opportunity.

Tweak Existing Marketing

Before starting anything new, take a look at what you've already got live. Make sure that it's building as much trust as it can, and that it fulfils The Conversation.

- Is all your current live material accurate?
- Have you used your trust marks where you can? These might be guarantees, review scores, customer testimonials, or anything else that builds The Conversation towards trust.
- Does it reflect your Editorial Mission Statement?
- Is there a tracking method in place for you to be able to see the results?

Auditing

After taking stock of your existing activities, divide each one over the three categories. What are you doing to Shine a Light? Target Customer and Get Found? Then score each of your activities out of five. Five points represents "We're doing everything we can", and zero means, "We're not doing anything here at all and we're missing a trick". This exercise will highlight where the gaps are, and filling the gaps is a great place to start – but what do you fill it with?

- What skills and connections do you have in your team?
- Would any of these methods be very easy for you to have a go at?

- What are you already doing? Have you angled it in the right way?
- Could you tweak anything you're doing to reach known customers in order to focus on the unknown potential customers as well?

This will give you a very simple view of where the opportunities and the easy starting points are.

Start with the category you are doing your worst in and the marketing method that you have the most existing skills and ability in.

If you're scoring low on all of it, start with the closest circle in – Get Found with those Google Shopping Campaigns!

Testing
Consolidate everything you've discovered so far into an easy-to-follow plan.

- What are you going to do? New marketing, and improvements to existing marketing.
- When are you going to do it?
- What's your performance expectation?
- How much budget can you put behind them?
- Who is going to be in charge of it?
- ...And anything else you think needs to be included.

Start following your plan, and as you get each bit working, add in your next potential new marketing methods. Keep optimizing. Optimizing never ends. Nothing is ever finished in this world of eCommerce! You've got to just keep tweaking and improving.

Website actions to attract the right Visitors to your website

Stage 1 is all about targeting the people who've never made it to your website, so there isn't much you need to do on your site for now.

There is some work you can do to make it easier for them to find you once they're ready to visit, and that involves tapping into the world of Search Engine Optimisation. I'm not going to be getting very in depth with that in this book because (a) a lot of it takes a long time before you see the results, (b) a lot of what I'm covering in later chapters will help with it anyway (e.g. content marketing) and (c) it's a big rabbit hole that we could easily disappear down for the next 20,000 words.[19]

Here are some simple website actions that will help your product pages and static content pages appear in the search engine rankings for the right things.

There are several straightforward things you can do to improve the SEO-ness of the pages on your website.

Much of the technicality that powers this is built into eCommerce systems, but sometimes you have to request it of your site builders. Whether it's already in place on your site or not, you need to understand it in order for it to make a difference for your business.

---

[19] You can read more about SEO in my book *eCommerce Marketing: How to Get Traffic that Buys to Your Website* – eCommerceMasterPlan.com/books.

These SEO tweaks are important because if someone is on a search engine searching for a product you sell, you want them to find you (yes, this can be seen as part of the Get Found marketing category too). These tweaks will make that much more likely because they make it easy for Google to realise what your page is about. If Google doesn't know what the page is about, they can't show it to people.

This is primarily about what is in the "tags" on your pages. "Tags" is shorthand for the HTML code used to mark things on your page as something special.

H1 Tags

The H1 tag signifies the most important text on the page. It should also be the text that best explains what's on the page. Therefore, there should only be one of them.

Usually, on a product page, it's the name of the product!

Usually, on a blog or article page, it's the name of the blog or article!

Check:

- The right headings on your pages are automatically being set as H1s.
- There is only one H1 tag on each page.
- You are writing product/page titles that explain your product – so "3 mugs" is bad, "A set of 3 plain blue mugs" is good.

Other H Tags

The H tags are not limited to the number 1. You can have lots of H tags – H2, H3, H4 and so on. The higher the number, the less important they show their content to be. Unlike the H1 tags, you can have multiples of each of these. Your second most important headings on the page should be H2, third most important headings H3, and so on.

To make these H tags super-powerful, you should include keywords from the H1 in them.

Sometimes there isn't anything you can set as H2, H3, and so on, and that's fine. However, most blogs and articles will benefit from subheadings because people like to scan – so you'll probably have some of these to set up.

Check:

- Are there subheadings on your page you would want set as other H tags?
- Are there new subheadings you should add and set up as H tags?
- Get those set up!

Images
With a few tweaks, you can explain your images much more clearly to the search engines and they'll be more likely to appear in search results. This will also help the search engine understand the whole page better, so it's not just about the image search results.

You should make sure your images have an ALT tag, a title, and a file name that match.

On a product page, you should set your tags to the name of the product it is showing. Some hosts will automatically do that for you as they process the images.

On a blog or article page, you should set your tags to describe the content of the image, and where possible include the keywords for the page.

Check:

- How are your images currently set up?
- Get them set up correctly!

Keyword Usage

Whilst the days of keyword stuffing are long dead, you do need to be focusing each page of your website on a keyword or keyphrase. For a product page, that is usually the name of or part of the name of the product!

Once you decide on a keyword or keyphrase, it should be used throughout the page (where it makes sense to put it). Adding it to the H1, images, and the other H tags will have helped.

You also need to include the keywords in the copy on the page, and include synonym phrases where possible.

Check:

- You've mentioned the name of the product in any copy on the page.
- Where you can, you've mentioned synonyms of the product name – as well as "crockery set" you've used "dinner set" and "set of plates and bowls".

Simple Metadata

Metadata is the general term for the all the things that can be wrapped up in all the tags I've talked about.

There are another two that, like image tags, can't be seen by the Visitors to your website, and which you'll want to get right.

The title tag is the tag that explains the title of your page. (You thought that was the H1? Well, almost, but no.) The only place you can see it on your website without going into the code is in the title bar of the browser:

The other place it appears is in the search results – most of the time, search engines will use your title tag as the big blue link in your listing.

So the title tag is really important to help the search engine know what your page is about AND encourage a customer to click to your website. Therefore, you want it to start with the name of the product or the blog post/article, and include your brand name at the end.

The meta description tag is the tag that describes what your page is about. No one can see it on your website, but it's usually the grey text that peters out on the search results.

On a product page you'll usually use the product description, or the first couple of paragraphs of the article or blog.

Check:

- On your product pages:
    - Your title tags are set to auto-fill with "{product name} – {your brand name}".
    - Your meta descriptions are set to auto-fill with "{product description}".
- On your static content pages:
    - Your title tags are set to auto-fill with "{page title} – {your brand name}".
    - Your meta descriptions are set to auto-fill with "{first 300 characters from the content}".

Stage 1: Attracting the Right Visitors

The Customer MasterPlan model works just like every process in the world – if you start off by adding bad things, you'll only get bad things out at the end. That means that the better a job you do of attracting the right people to your website, the easier (in effort, money, stress, and profit!) it will be to grow your business.

You don't just want lots of Visitors, you want good quality Visitors. To get them, you need to create the right marketing messages and put it front of the right people, using the right marketing methods.

Stage 1 is a Stage where no action is ever finished – you will have to keep analysing the research, and optimising the marketing methods.

Because this Stage is never finished, please don't think you have to implement everything in this chapter on day one. It's a very long chapter with lots of ideas, and it could easily take you a whole year to do it all. Start with what's easy for you, and those areas that you believe will make the biggest difference for your business the fastest.

You'll have seen with some of the case studies I've outlined that other business owners are only using one or two of these methods to get things moving, then making sure they're doing something with those Visitors to turn them into Enquirers and Buyers.

You're going to be coming back to this Stage again and again, so please don't try and do it all at once. Rather, put some great activity live, watch the right customers land on your website and work on Stage 2 and 3 to make sure you are converting those Visitors into Buyers.

5 Stage 2: Turning Visitors into Enquirers

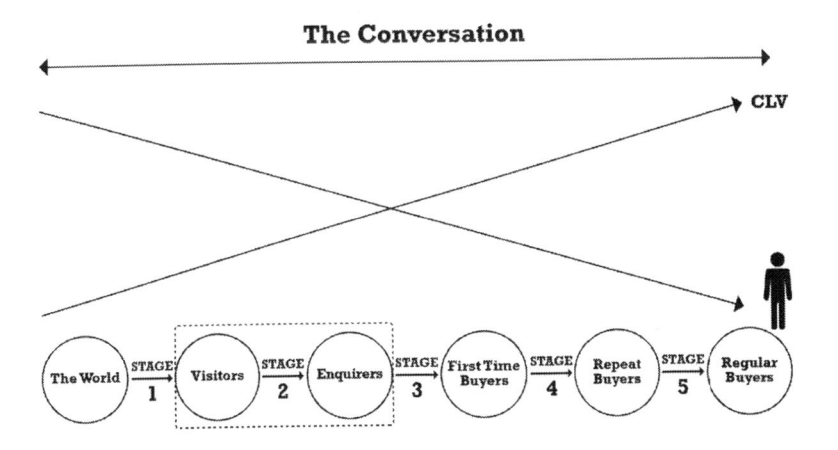

The Conversation

CLV

The World — STAGE 1 → Visitors — STAGE 2 → Enquirers — STAGE 3 → First Time Buyers — STAGE 4 → Repeat Buyers — STAGE 5 → Regular Buyers

STAGE 2 is all about getting the email sign up. It's about taking those customers who have visited the website and getting them to hand over their email address.

Customer Persuasion | 97

It's a very important part of The Customer MasterPlan because:

- It's the first time during The Conversation that you get something of value from the effort you've put in – the email address.
- It's the first time you get to interact with the customer on your turf – they've come to your website.
- It's the first time you're talking to those who you know have some interest in your business

Often businesses make the mistake of aiming for the purchase and forgetting everything that should come before it. That's why I have devoted a whole Stage simply to getting the email address. However, this Stage is not about forcing a customer to give their email address before they are allowed to buy. Customers will sometimes leapfrog the sign up step and go straight to purchase – that is fine.

If you're tempted to ignore this Stage and just go straight to getting the first purchase, please don't! Much of this Stage also helps get the sale. If you still need more convincing... have a look at the following case studies.[20]

---

[20] Each of these is a business I've interviewed on my podcast, so you can hear them all in more detail at: eCommerceMasterPlan.com/podcast.

Project Repat

"It's all about collecting the emails."

Nathan Rothstein and his partner Ross Lohr launched Project Repat to turn their customer's old t-shirts into blankets. In 2015, they turned over $4 million.

Their strategy mirrors The Customer MasterPlan – when someone gets to their website, they focus on building The Conversation and getting that email address.

Optimising this process has increased their email sign up rate to 8% of Visitors. Their welcome programme (which we'll cover in the next chapter) turns up to 25% of them into customers.

There's more about Project Repat in the next chapter.

Wet Shave Club

Rohan Gilkes runs WetShaveClub.com, an online-only business with a big subscription side. In year one, they turned over $350,000 from their tribe of 20,000.

Gathering email addresses was a key to their growth. Initially they got just 50 sign ups a month with a rather passive pop up. After several months of testing and optimising, the pop ups grew sign ups to 600 a month in late 2015, converting about 8% of their Visitors.

There's more about Wet Shave Club in Chapter 8.

Miso Tasty

We've already heard about Bonnie Chung and MisoTasty.com (best business name ever). For Bonnie's business to keep growing, she needs to continue The Conversation from their great PR coverage and retail placement through email newsletters. It takes a fair bit to convince someone to try a new type of food, and do it online, so she credits her email sign up as key to getting customers to try out her product. There's more about that in coming chapters.

What's the aim of Stage 2?

The aim of this Stage is to get the customers who've visited your website to give you their email address.

To do that, you have to continue building on The Conversation that started with your marketing in Stage 1, and continue building their trust in your business.

To achieve the aim, it's also really important to give a clear "sign up!" CTA to the customers who've visited the site. If you don't ask, you won't get.

Strange things happen in Stage 2: Customers may leapfrog

This is the only Stage where customers can (and will!) leapfrog a Stage. You will have customers who come to your website or store for the first time and buy, going straight from being a Visitor to being a First Time Buyer.

That's awesome!

This chapter is purely about getting the email address, not getting the sale (that's in the next chapter).

Strange things happen in Stage 2: Customers may go back and forth

It may take a few visits to your website before a customer is ready to part with their email address, or sees the call to action that leads them to do it. This means they're going to yo-yo backwards and forwards between Stage 1 and Stage 2 activity.

How does The Conversation fit into this Stage?

In this Stage, The Conversation is quite passive. You build the message into the content and design on the website, but you're not putting big "look at me" marketing pieces out there.

Don't make the mistake of thinking "passive" means unimportant. You still need to make sure everything that's on your site fits with your Editorial Mission and The Conversation you're building.

Here, The Conversation is talking to customers who've come to your website for the first time. They've experienced enough of The Conversation to want to visit your website, you've started building trust with them, and now their visit to your website will either:

1. Confirm that trust was well placed, leaving the customer with positive thoughts and emotions towards you.

2. Show the opposite of what your marketing suggested, so your relationship with that customer has moved into one of distrust, and they will be hard-pushed to return.

3. Prove your business to be even more trustworthy than you appeared from your marketing, leading the customer to think, "Wow, I must give this business my email address!".

Obviously you're aiming for the third option!

The key things to convey with The Conversation in Stage 2 are:

- We are a real business.
- Our customers love us.
- Our products are great.
- This is who we are.
- This is what we sell.
- These are our values.
- We know lots about our subject.

You'll see many of these points overlap with Stage 1, and that's no accident. You're still building their knowledge and awareness of the business. Customers of all levels will keep experiencing your Stage 1 and Stage 2 (and Stage 3, and so on) marketing – neither a press article nor the trust marks on your site will be seen exclusively on a first or last visit. That is why consistency is a critical component of building trust.

During this Stage, the message of The Conversation is conveyed both in first impressions and first glance positioning, AND in longer content pieces.

Yes, it's quite a bit of work to get The Conversation conveyed correctly for this Stage.

The good news is that everything you do to increase the power of The Conversation in Stage 2 will improve your business's relationship with every single customer who comes to your website, whichever customer level they've reached.

What can my customers teach me about what I should be doing at this Stage?

We've already covered a lot about how you can identify the powerful messages to get customers to your website. Hold onto those for this Stage as well (you'll find the details back in Chapters 3 and 4).

For this Stage, customers can also tell you where on your site the effort should be focused.

- Which pages do customers first arrive on your website from?
- Which pages do they look at before they leave?

The rest of The Conversation work for this Stage is fairly standard across all businesses, so you don't need to learn a lot from your existing customers in order to improve the outcomes at this Stage. Great news if you're just starting out!

Required research and prep work

Your website undoubtedly has hundreds (if not thousands) of pages. Spending time improving the first impression created by every single one of those would be a waste of effort that could be more profitably expended elsewhere.

In this Stage, your research is all about working out where the effort is best spent.

What is the first page most customers see on the website?

To make a good first impression, it's important to know where that first impression happens. For many customers who land on your website, the homepage will the first thing they see, but there may be other pages that are also important.

Google Analytics can provide this information very easily. Sign in to Analytics and head to Behaviour > Site Content > Landing Pages.

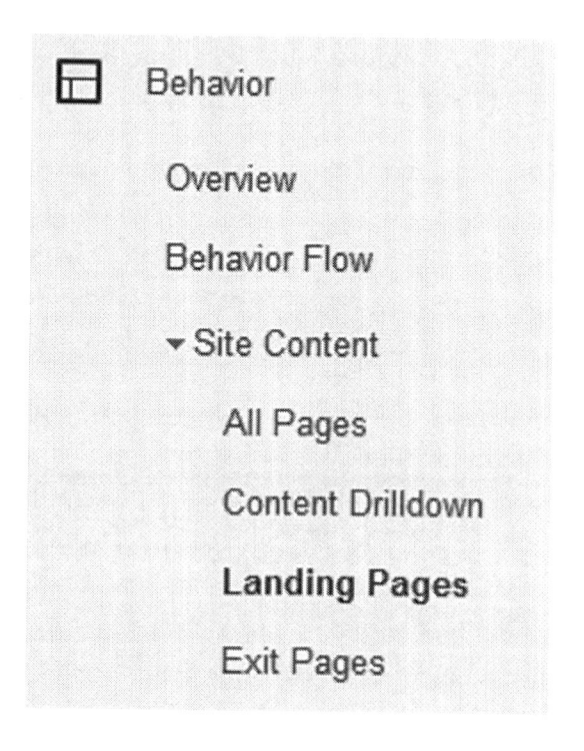

```
Behavior
    Overview
    Behavior Flow
    ▼ Site Content
        All Pages
        Content Drilldown
        Landing Pages
        Exit Pages
```

Put in a timespan that will give you some reasonable data. I recommend you start with three months.

Stage 2: Turning Visitors into Enquirers | 105

Landing Page		Acquisition			Behavior		
		Sessions	% New Sessions	New Users	Bounce Rate	Pages / Session	Avg. Session Duration
		5,164 % of Total 100.00% (5,164)	68.75% Avg for View: 68.73% (0.03%)	3,550 % of Total 100.03% (3,549)	71.55% Avg for View: 71.55% (0.00%)	1.69 Avg for View: 1.69 (0.00%)	00:01:40 Avg for View: 00:01:40 (0.00%)
1.	/	961 (18.61%)	68.47%	658 (18.54%)	40.58%	2.50	00:02:30
2.	/the-7-ecommerce-business-structures/	906 (17.54%)	90.18%	817 (23.01%)	91.83%	1.13	00:00:38
3.	/podcast/	276 (5.34%)	57.25%	158 (4.45%)	44.93%	2.56	00:03:47
4.	/sign-up-for-updates-from-the-ecommerce-masterplan/thank-you-for-signing-up-to-our-emails/	163 (3.16%)	0.61%	1 (0.03%)	50.92%	2.12	00:01:25
5.	/ecommerce-delivery/	127 (2.46%)	90.55%	115 (3.24%)	91.34%	1.17	00:00:29
6.	/contact/	122 (2.36%)	68.85%	84 (2.37%)	74.59%	1.72	00:00:55
7.	/automating-pinterest-how-to-schedule-your-pins/	79 (1.53%)	93.67%	74 (2.08%)	92.41%	1.13	00:00:29

This is our landing page data for eCommerceMasterPlan.com, showing the pages that most customers see when they land on the website. In analysing this data, you should be looking at:

- The number of sessions, which indicates how important it is to get that page right.

- The three behaviour stats (Bounce Rate, Pages/Session, and Average Session Duration) indicate how well that page is doing to keep customers interested and on the website. Note that the Bounce Rate should be low, but the Pages/Session and Average Session Duration should be high.

- What you know about those pages – sometimes odd things get thrown up. See below for some examples.

(Warning: Please don't take the numbers above as benchmarks – benchmark against your own site, the numbers in the top row. Obviously, better than your average is good and worse is bad.)

Here's what my business can learn from this, line by line:

Line 1: The homepage
It's doing a great job! All three behaviour stats are much better than the average scores for my website.

- Bounce rate: 40.58% vs. 71.55%
- Pages / Session: 2.50 vs. 1.69
- Average Session Duration: 2 minutes 30 seconds vs. 1m 40s

Line 2: The "7 eCommerce business structures" page
It's not doing very well, but it's not the fault of the page.

I know this is a page that gets LOTS of new traffic from Google. And from diving into that, I know that most of the customers Google drives to this page are looking for information about how to structure an eCommerce team. That's not what this page covers. Instead it details the different routes to market for an eCommerce business, a theory explained in *eCommerce MasterPlan: Your 3 Steps to Successful Online Selling*.[21]

To improve the performance here, I'd need to rename my theory, rewrite the book, move the content on this page to another page using the new theory title, and then write something for this page about team structure. I may yet do that, but it's not a priority for Stage 2!

Line 3: The Podcast page
Looking good – it's the second best for engagement after the homepage, and it's my third most popular landing page, but look

---

[21] You can find out how to get a copy at: eCommerceMasterPlan.com/books.

how much the Sessions volume has dropped off. We've gone from being in the 900s to the 200s – that's over 60% less traffic, which means at the moment this is a much less important page.

Behaviour stats are great, lots of interaction on all fronts.

A lot of our marketing points customers to this page, so it's great to see good engagement levels.

Line 4: Thank you page

We're not going to learn a lot from this one as it's another anomaly.

This is the "thank you" page that customers see after they sign up, and it comes up because they sometimes go via a third party website to get to that page. So as far as the customer is concerned, it wasn't the first page they went to on the website.

Line 5: The "eCommerce Delivery" book page

This is the page where Visitors can find out how to buy the *eCommerce Delivery* book. It's not a page we do a lot of marketing about, so it's a surprise to see it in this top seven landing pages.

It's got pretty terrible behaviour numbers, but at this point the volume of sessions has dropped down to just 127 so it's not a huge concern.

There's definitely more that we could be doing with this page, but selling copies of this book isn't a high priority at the moment.

Line 6: The "Contact Us" page

It's surprising to see that one in here too.

Only 122 sessions, but the behaviour stats show a mixed message:

- Bounce rate: 74.59% vs. 71.55% — not that far from average.
- Pages/Session: 1.72 vs. 1.69 — better than average, but very similar.
- Average Session Duration: only 55s vs. 1m 40s — way off the average.

This is a page where a sign up form would fit nicely, as Visitors to this page are looking to get in contact with us, so I think I'll add an email sign up to it.

Line 7: A blog post about automating Pinterest pins
Very similar stats to the "Delivery" book page.

The session volume is very low.

For your analysis, you could drill down further by focusing purely on the new sessions and new user numbers, or even segment the data to only show first time Visitors. However, some customers will come back several times before signing up, so I think it's much more useful to look at the landing page data as a whole. Plus, more data means more accurate interpretations.

From this analysis, I now know which pages I need to care about. My research is done, and I can go on to see what actions to take with this information to get more email sign ups.

Website actions to turn Visitors into Enquirers

In this Stage, the great majority of your work is on the website itself and not on your marketing channels.

This section covers the groundwork on the website to build up The Conversation and that all-important trust, getting Visitors ready to sign up. In the next section, you will see how to ask for the sign up.

Building The Conversation: First impressions count

Stage 1 lays down a lot of work to get customers to the website. That first impression they get must:

- Show your business to be trustworthy.
- Back up the messages (The Conversation) given out during the marketing that got them to the website.

One website I frequently want to click through to from Facebook is The West Briton, my local newspaper in Cornwall, but their site is so full of advertising that it's a painful experience to use on a desktop, let alone on a mobile. This is an example of a business that doesn't understand how to build the same levels of trust throughout their Conversation. (If you want to check it out, go to www.westbriton.co.uk or www.facebook.com/westbriton/, although I recommend you don't!)

Here are the things every site should do to be seen as trustworthy.

Be Up-To-Date

The design needs to look like something from this decade, not the last decade. If the design doesn't scream "up-to-date", then customers assume nothing about the site is, which erodes trust.

You also need to make sure any messages are current. By the first day of January, your Christmas messages should no longer be on the website.

PLEASE make sure your © statement doesn't show last year, as it immediately makes you look out-of-date.

Appear Active

If you're feeding Twitter posts or blog posts onto the homepage (or the other landing pages you've identified), make sure there's something there from within the last month. If there isn't, write something or turn the feed off on that page.

Live chat can also really help with this.

Prove You're Real

Again, live chat helps, especially if it includes an employee's name.

Welcome to LiveChat

Jenna
Reservations

Jenna

Welcome back! Can our reservations team help you with anything today?

Include your company contact details (a legal requirement in parts of Europe) including:

- Phone number
- Address (office and warehouse if different)
- Email or contact form

It's often a great idea to really shout about the fact customers can contact you – like Bureau Direct are doing here in the header:

We're here to help! Call 020 8834 4700

You can tweak the CTA to add to show more of your character and further improve The Conversation, like Classic Sailing (classic-sailing.co.uk) does with their text, "Ask a Skipper".

You should include links to active social media profiles. If you're willing to spend time on social media, you're probably a serious business, and it makes it easy for them to check you out.

Show Customers' Trust
If you can show that other customers trust you, the new Visitor is more likely to trust you. Humans care what other humans think!

This could be in the form of customer testimonials and reviews, an image of a review on the homepage, a quote in the header, or a feed from your review software. It can be as simple or complex as you want to make it.

112 | Customer Persuasion

Here, Beads Direct (beadsdirect.co.uk) put them right in their homepage and show very recent ones. This screengrab is from the 16th February 2016.

If you have a review system in place, add the overall score prominently – ideally on every page of the website by using it in the footer or the header.

CUSTOMER TESTIMONIALS   READ MORE >

DONNA
09 FEB 2016
Ordered Sunday night and they were delivered before Tuesday afternoon. Thank you for the Æ£10 voucher and my 25% discount by joining the VIP Club. I love your beads!!!!

DIANE DICKENSON
09 FEB 2016
I will be making Beads Direct my first port of call in future.

JENNIFER GRACIE
08 FEB 2016
I would highly recommend Beads Direct to everyone. They have amazing products and more than happy to help with any issues when making any type of jewellery. Customer service is brilliant and the way every company should be. Keep up the great work and look forward to buying more in the near future.

Beads Direct use it right in their header.[22]

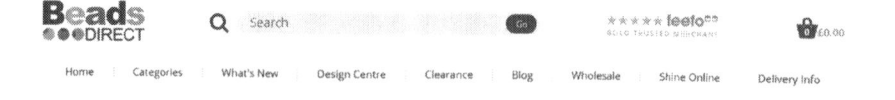

Beads DIRECT   Search   Go   ★★★★★ feefo   £0.00
Home | Categories | What's New | Design Centre | Clearance | Blog | Wholesale | Shine Online | Delivery Info

This would also be the time to flag if you're the number one in your sector, as that shows LOTS of people trust you.

Show Organisations' Trust
If other organisations (news sources, businesses, etc.) have shown trust in you, customers who trust them are more likely to trust you!

---

22   A fascinating business – hear the podcast episode at: eCommerceMasterPlan.com/podcast.

News Sources

Include on the site which news sources you've been featured in.

Here's the list from At Home in the Country's homepage.

Note how almost all of them fit really well with their core customer base: people who live in the country and love hunting, shooting, fishing, and tweed.

In quite a different marketplace, Nineteenth Amendment does the same on their "More Information" page[23].

Awards

Any award (even if you don't think your customers will care) will help prove your business is trustworthy. It might be a local award, one for you as a great entrepreneur, or a national business award. Put it clearly on those important landing pages.

Bureau Direct (bureaudirect.com) display their awards in their footer, using their series of ECMOD awards to show they are

---

23 Another of our podcast guests: eCommerceMasterPlan.com/podcast.

114 | Customer Persuasion

consistently good, and their Trustpilot award to show their customers love them.[24]

AWARD WINNING STORE

The good news on the awards front is that your suppliers know that your business will benefit from awards, and that handing them out is a great way to build a strong relationship, so there's ever more of them up for grabs.

The bad news is that it means you need to win multiple awards to get the same benefit you would have got just a few years ago from one award.

Important Customers
There might also be great organisations or famous individuals who you are lucky enough to have as a customer, either a directly or through wholesale.

Deborah Lippmann (deborahlippmann.com) does this really well on the homepage to show both her celebrity manicure portfolio and the key department stores that stock her nail varnishes.[25]

---

24 One of our most popular podcast episodes of 2016 was with Bureau Direct. You can listen right here at: eCommerceMasterPlan.com/podcast.
25 Really interesting interview available at: eCommerceMasterPlan.com/podcast.

Stage 2: Turning Visitors into Enquirers | 115

EXPLORE DEBORAH'S CELEBRITY MANICURIST PORTFOLIO

Sephora . Barneys New York . Nordstrom . Neiman Marcus

Here's the list that At Home In the Country show on their "About Us" page (I'd add it to the homepage as well).

We also supply our products to some of the finest Palaces, Castles, Country Houses, Hotels and businesses in the UK.

IN ENGLAND :- Hampton Court, Kensington Palace, Blenheim Palace, Sandringham, Haddon Hall, Rockingham Castle, Rothschild Waddesdon Manor, Longleat, Bamburgh Castle, Alnwick Castle, Castle Howard, The National Horse Racing Museum, Farlows of Picadilly, Garden Centres and independent retailers all over the country.

IN SCOTLAND :- Balmoral, Glamis Castle, Scone Palace, Floors Castle, Inverary Castle, Ballindalloch Castle, Cawdor Castle, Blair Castle, Edinburgh Castle, Stirling Castle, The Royal Yacht Britannia, Gleneagles Hotel, The House of Bruar, The House of Darrach, The Duck Bay Hotel, Gleneagles Hotel, William Glen, the list goes on and on...!

IN WALES :- Eastnor Castle (Near Wales!) Charlie's Stores and many other Garden Centres and independent retailers.

Now that is QUITE the list!

But Donald Russell (donaldrussell.com), a UK-based butcher's, trump that completely.

116 | Customer Persuasion

DONALD RUSSELL
Real food, real flavour, every day

MEAT   POULTRY & GAME   SEAFOOD   READY MEALS   WINTER

That crest to the left of the logo is called a Royal Warrant and has been awarded to them by the Queen. The text states, "By Appointment to Her Majesty the Queen supplier of meat and poultry Donald Russell Limited Inverurie".

They reinforce this message on their homepage banners.

- Traditionally hand prepard using our premium, juicy pork
- Top quality - just like you'd expect from a Royal Warrant holding butcher!
- Plus delicious NEW speciality sausages to try, inspired by the Continent...

All the text on this banner is giving the Visitor a reason to trust them.

Now, not many businesses are able to add a Royal Warrant to their website, but ask yourself – who already trusts you? Who or what can you name on your website to show that others should trust you?

Offer a Guarantee
A guarantee should show the customer that if they buy and something goes wrong, you're going to solve the problem for them.

In most countries there is a legal period of time in which someone can return goods – you can just turn this into a Guarantee statement and logo. Why not? You have to comply with it anyway.

Depending on your product category, you may need or want to take it further.

Warren Evans (warrenevans.com) sells beds and mattresses. They have lots of awards, reviews, and other trust marks. They also offer every customer a "120 Night Mattress Trial", so the customer can sleep on their mattress for a couple of months to make sure it's the right one for them. That really shows they care.

Turtle Mat (turtlemat.co.uk) offer a 5-year guarantee on all their door mats. When a customer sees a guarantee of that length, they know they're getting a quality product.

Security
Showing you care about security is an easy but hugely important step. Even if you're a start-up with no notable customers, press coverage, or reviews (yet), you can put up these trust marks on your website.

All of these have a positive impact on a customer's trust, and help make it really clear you are a website that sells things! Include:

- The logos of the credit cards and payment methods you take.
    - Visa, Mastercard, American Express, etc.
    - PayPal, Amazon, Apple Pay, etc.
    - Bitcoin, etc.
- The logos of the security tools you're using.
    - Sage Pay, etc.
    - Verisign, etc.

Here's Beads Direct again. They have this in their footer:

You could also add a "Google Certified Shop" logo.

Cohesion

This one's a bit harder to tick off the list. It means that nothing jars or vexes the customer during their experience of your business.

The experience should be the same on all platforms, and each platform appears cohesively. There shouldn't be ten different fonts fighting for attention on the homepage!

This includes the site working on mobile and tablet too.

Those are the quick wins on the website. Whilst they definitely are wins, if you really want to maximise the chances of someone giving you their email address, you need to look at some of the bigger content pieces.

Building The Conversation: Adding longer and customer-generated content

All those logos and promotional text snippets will build trust with the Visitor, but they might not be enough to get them to give you their email address. So you need to add a bit more colour to your business with some longer content.

This could be anywhere on your site, from product pages to homepage, from FAQ to your blog. First I'll cover the general themes, and then I'm going to go into a few key pages you really MUST get right.

What Content?

Just what sort of content are we talking about? All content that's on your website, which might be read by any Visitor, whatever Level they are at. Your focus in this Stage is on the Visitors – giving them what they need to know about you, your business and your products. Basically, continuing The Conversation on the website.

This content exists to build a trusting relationship between your business and your customers. The stronger the relationship, the more likely customers are to convert (that's either signing up or buying, moving from one Stage to the next). That's because the more they know about you and your business, the more they'll trust you, and people like to do business with those they trust. This content puts something of a human face on the business, giving it more character and making it easier to relate to.

It also lifts the curtain a bit, showing them more about your products and services, and how your business works.

It's going to help the Visitor understand if you're going to give them what they're looking for. It helps them work out if they're a good fit as a customer of your business, which has the added bonus of pulling the good fit customers closer to you. It's also going to encourage those who aren't a good fit to go elsewhere, if yours aren't the products they're looking for or if yours isn't the philosophy they're looking for.

Of course, fundamentally, the fewer unanswered questions there are or the easier it is to find answers, the more likely someone is to trust you. If they can't find an answer they want, the immediate reaction of a human is to start assuming you're hiding something from them. Your aim with all this content is to avoid this situation and answer every possible question they've got.

Types of Content

There's a range of content types that can sit on your site and answer your Visitors' questions.

Written

This could be a blog, something in your articles, an About Us, or a delivery page.

Written content can encompass everything from FAQs and buyer's guides, to a product selection diary by your head buyer, or the product descriptions on your pages.

Video
You could feature diary style videos, face-to-camera, product demos, or catwalk shows of the new collection.

Images
Photos of your team are great at showing a human side, or behind-the-scenes shots of what's going on.

Depending on your products, you might have infographics to help explain key facts about the products and maybe even compare them. Which one is suitable for which scenario?

Audio
Audio is the least used and the least obvious. One good example comes from ASOS, the fast fashion brand who are now running a podcast of their own.

Anna Halsall, Urbello founder, talks turning a daydream into a big business

If you've been a guest on a podcast, then embed it. Get the code to put the player on your site so customers can click play right on your website. You could include this in a blog post or on your "About Us" page.

This is a great way to both promote your business for Stage 1, and use the same activity to build trust in Stage 2.

The good thing is there are endless ways you can use these different forms of content on your website. There's sure to be something that suits your products, your customers' needs, and your team's abilities, which means there's no point in banging your head against a brick wall with a content format you just can't stand producing. Move on to something else, find something that works for you and create that content. What needs to come through is the passion, the enthusiasm, and the desire to help your customers.

Where to Put Content

There are key areas on your website where this content could go.

Static and Information Pages

On different systems, these can be called different things. These are the pages you usually list in the footer or on a customer services menu. Stuff like delivery information, "About Us", "Contact Us", returns, and FAQs quite often sit here.

These are the pages which are permanently in existence and which give the Visitor to your website really critical information they need to know.

These pages need to exist, answer all the customer's questions, and represent you as a business. It's got to be on brand, clear, accurate, up-to-date, and easy to find and use.

Part of making sure it's easy to find is not getting too creative with the names of these pages – try to stick to the same titles everyone else is using. So "Frequently Asked Questions", "Delivery", "Returns", "About Us", Contact Us". It's not very exciting – but it's good for the customer because it makes it easy for them to find what they're looking for.

FAQ pages can become a bit of a nightmare if you only have the one, so quite often they end up needing a navigation system. It might also include information like buying guides. For example, if you're selling mattresses you need some permanent information up there to explain what to look for in a mattress, and what might suit each customer best.

Much of the information on these pages is related to buying, and whilst that's not the aim of this Stage, Visitors may well be checking it out before they decide to sign up.

Evolving Content Pages
Usually this will be in the form of a blog, but please don't get hung up on the technicalities of the terminology. Some web or content management systems don't have a blog, but do allow you to create articles that look and behave like a blog.

A blog is a piece of content that at some point may go out-of-date, but you don't need to worry about that. They're kind of like an archive of news updates.

Think of this as being like your customer magazine. This is where you announce a new season, show behind the scenes, shout about PR success, and embed the podcast you just appeared on. It's also where you explore a product category in depth.

Your static information pages should always be up-to-date. Your evolving content pages will pass through the mist of time and go out-of-date.

It's important to note that I'm definitely not suggesting you create content for the sake of content. How much content you need to create depends on how much your Visitors need to know before they trust you enough to sign up or buy.

The "About Us" Page
Getting all this content right and live is a never-ending task, because your products, business, and the customers' requirements keep evolving. I recommend setting aside half a day per week to work on this until you've got things up-to-date, and plan to regularly set aside another chunk of time to maintain everything. Start with the "About Us" Page.

Make this interesting and representative of your business' identity. Show some skin, pictures of the real team doing real things. Not too much – I'm not talking about getting a photoshoot done. I mean taking your phone around the business and taking some pictures of people working at desks, picking and packing, the reality of what goes on from day-to-day, because that's what you're trying to show. If you have a compelling founder story, put that in. You don't need a biography of every single member of the team unless of course it fits with your brand identity. This is your opportunity to show the human side of the business.

I should also point out this is a really hard one to create. You may never be happy with it. You will probably go through many incarnations before you're even vaguely happy with it, and that's absolutely fine. But trust me, your worst attempt is far better than just the legal company information and your address.

You may well be coming back to the "About Us" page again and again and again, but at least get something decent up there.

Website Actions to obtain email addresses

Given the whole point of this Stage is about getting the enquiry, this section is all about how to maximise the likelihood of getting the email address from your Visitors.

The basics

Hopefully you've got this stuff covered already.

Ask

I know that sounds really obvious, but you'd be surprised how many websites I look at where I can't work out how to sign up.

I want to sign up to their emails, often from a professional standpoint of wanting to see what they are up to, but with some websites it's like pulling teeth trying to work out where to add my email address.

Make sure you've asked for it somewhere. If you don't ask, you're not going to get.

Use the Footer

SIGN UP FOR THE LATEST NEWS, BE THE FIRST IN THE KNOW.

Sign up to our newsletter to be among the first to get the latest Maxwell Scott Bags news, product launches, behind the scenes and much more.

[✉ enter email]   [SUBMIT]

(f) (twitter) (p) (instagram) (t) (youtube)

This is a great way to make it easy to get that sign up. It's always there, on every page of your site, it's clear, and it's somewhere customers will expect to find a sign up form. Make sure that sign up form appears in the footer.

Use More than One Place

Put your sign up form everywhere it's relevant. That might well be on the "Contact Us" page, on your "About Us" page, or anywhere you can add a note to "find out more about us, subscribe to our emails".

There are places around the site where it makes sense to add these in, so make sure that you've put it in multiple places if and where it makes sense to do so.

A lot of email systems will enable you to track the different sign up forms in different places, so you can see which places give you more sign ups.

It's always good to make sure you've got your email sign up in multiple places because customers look for it in different places, and are motivated to sign up by different types of content and messages.

Easy Forms
If you pre-filled those boxes with 'email address' and 'your name' and that kind of stuff, make sure this filler text disappears the second they click on it.

Make sure your sign up form works on mobiles and on tablets. If it doesn't, turn it off on those devices. Otherwise you're just giving customers a terrible user experience, which is going to erode all that great work you've done in The Conversation to build trust with the customer.

Minimal Information
We've all encountered those email sign up forms where you're asked to give them your first name, last name, email address, postcode, country, tick five boxes, spin around three times, and then click four buttons.

Please don't do that.

At this point, the aim is only to get the email.

Once you've got the email, you can then work on getting all the other desirable information, and the moment someone buys from you you're going to get it anyway.

At most, you should be asking for their name and their email address. But if you can manage it, try and just ask for the email. I should say that at eCommerceMasterPlan.com, we ask for a first name and an email because we immediately personalise a lot of our follow up emails.

If you're desperate to get extra information out of customers, do a two-Stage sign up. Many assume that no one will fill in the second Stage, but actually it's not uncommon to get over 80% of sign ups filling in the second form too.

This means that the sign up form asks for a name and email, or just an email address. The "thank you" page they land on after they filled in that form asks for more information. For example, it may be you take them to a page that asks for a postal address for the purpose of sending something in the post. Direct Marketing using the postal system remains a very powerful way to get a customer to respond, so don't assume you're limited to online marketing methods.

Automatic System

If you, or someone on your team, has to manually log into the website or download a spreadsheet before uploading new sign ups to your email system, it's damaging your business on two fronts.

1. It's slowing down the natural flow of The Conversation and letting the customer down, because there will be a delay in them giving you their information and getting what you've promised them.

2. It will have a negative impact on sign up volumes because it creates a psychological barrier. If every email sign up you get gives you more work to do, it doesn't inspire or encourage you to want more sign ups.

You don't have to be on an especially clever or expensive email marketing platform to be able to do this. Pretty much every option out there will do this for you now, from Mail Chimp upwards.

Be Trustworthy

Have a safe data statement right there in your email sign up form. What I mean by that is a statement about respecting data and a promise not to abuse it. It might say "we care about your data, we promise to never spam you", or "we promise not to give your data to a third party". It only needs to be a one-liner.

You might want to accompany it with a padlock icon sitting right by the sign up button. This will give customers the reassurance that you care about their data and how you're going to use it.

Clear Privacy Policy

This is also about being trustworthy. Some customers won't believe that little safe data statement gives them the whole picture, and they will want to go and read the privacy policy.

Don't link to it from the form itself, because that's creating clutter. The clearer that form is, the more likely the potential customer will sign up, but do make sure your privacy policy is accessible and up-to-date. Make sure it's representative of what you're actually doing, and that there is a clear link to it on your website. If Visitors can't find it, they'll assume you're hiding something whether or not you actually are.

Using messages and incentives

Every sign up is a transaction – the Visitor is giving you their email address in return for something. So you need to give them a reason to sign up, something in return for their email.

It might be a simple promise or an incentive. There are three types of incentives you can use, based on the different outcomes you are aiming for.

I recommend you start with a simple promise and get a benchmark sign up to conversion rate, then test other ideas against that benchmark.

Promise Something

You need to promise that you're going to give them something in return for their email address. I know there's no money changing hands, but there is a transaction taking place.

The promise itself doesn't need to be huge.

We're not necessarily talking incentives of monetary value; we're talking about promises such as, "You'll hear the latest news about new products and discounts!". It doesn't need to be complicated. It might just be, "Find out everything that's going on behind the scenes", but do make sure that whatever you're promising is something you're actually going to deliver.

Here's a nice one from Buttermilk (buttermilk.co.uk):

And another example from Donald Russell:

FANCY ANOTHER BITE?

Subscribe to our mailing list for mouth-watering exclusive online offers, nifty chef's tips and cooking guides, recipes and even videos...

Enter Email Address

SUBSCRIBE

Don't promise a weekly newsletter full of tips, competitions, and behind the scenes footage if (a) you don't have any behind the scenes footage, (b) you don't have any competitions planned and (c) you're not going to be sending it weekly. This will cause you problems down the line!

Promise something you're actually going to deliver. If it helps, think of a reason why they'd want to sign up and what they'd want to hear from your business.

Incentivise the First Purchase
This is an incentive to get someone to make their first purchase.

132 | Customer Persuasion

Here's an example from Nineteenth Amendment.[26] They offer both a promise and $19 off the first order if you give them your email address.

NINETEENTH AMENDMENT

INDEPENDENT. DESIGNER. PRE-SALES.

Signup and get **$19.00** toward your first purchase!

Get free, exclusive access to the next big names in fashion from around the globe.

E-MAIL

Enter your email address

PASSWORD

Enter Your Password

GO

OR

LOGIN WITH FACEBOOK

Already a member? Login here.

Bureau Direct, have "Stationery Wednesday", a monthly, one-week, 10%-off discount for everyone on their newsletter list.[27]

NEWSLETTER SIGN UP   10% Off Orders for Subscribers >>   your name   Email address   subscribe

---

26 You can listen to Nineteenth Amendment's interview in full at eCommerceMasterPlan.com/podcast.
27 You can listen to Bureau Direct interview in full at eCommerceMasterPlan.com/podcast.

Beads Direct offer a simple promise and a discount in their exit pop-up.[28]

15% OFF WHEN YOU SIGN UP!

Before you go, why not subscribe to our newsletter and you'll be the first to hear about our latest news, discounts and offers.

Your Email Address

Sign up

No thanks, I would like to continue shopping

Here I'm talking maybe a P&P freebie, a discount, or a free gift with an order. Any incentive that can only be realised when a customer places an order.

Competitions
This is an example of something you can do just to get that sign up, whether the prize is gift vouchers, discounts, or free products.

---

28   You can listen to Beads Direct interview in full at eCommerceMasterPlan.com/podcast.

It could be a competition using your own products, or you could try a competition using someone else's product as the prize.

Not many businesses use competitions, not least because it can be harder to manage than a simple offer and customers tend to respond less well. However, give it a test with your business to see how it works for you.

Continuing The Conversation
This is where rather than offer money or a promise, you're giving away something which builds The Conversation. Maybe a free training course, a free download, a free pdf, or another piece of content to get the customer understanding more about your business.

Essentially you need to find the incentive that fits best with your business and brand. At this point, it's not "one size fits all".

There is also the warning here that if you create too amazing a reason to sign up, you may get an awful lot of bad data signing up. "Bad data" is a person who signs up for the prize or offer, but isn't interested in your business. This lower quality data will cost you money to engage with and is very unlikely to become a customer, let alone a repeat customer. This is why you've really got to keep everything you're giving away in line with your over-all brand, so it attracts the right customers to sign up.

Whilst working on this book, I came across this fascinating pop-up incentive on thehustle.co:

> "Oh shit... another popup. Hurry up and click the X so you can keep on reading."
>
> **Wait, just wait a second.**
>
> You're already reading this so you might as well let me finish my point. Look, you came to this site because you saw something cool. Most likely it was on your Facebook feed or that blog you always read.
>
> But here's the deal. This site, also known as The Hustle, is actually a biweekly newsletter. We only post some of our stuff online so people like you can randomly come across it and find out about us. So, if you like what you're reading, enter your email here. Then, if you like our emails, we both win. If you don't like it we'll Venmo you $1. Try it.
>
> *Enter your email address*

I really like this one because:

- It's full of character. It supports their Editorial Mission and builds The Conversation.
- There's some humour in the first line.
- They make a great case for why a Visitor should want to sign up.
- They offer a guarantee that the Visitor will like the emails, or the Visitor will get a $1 gift.

Pop-Ups

When I say pop-up, I mean an email sign up form that isn't part of your standard website. It could be:

- An interstitial.
- In a header or footer banner.
- A pop-up.
- An exit pop-up.
- An overlay.

I don't really care about the terminology you use, I care about the fact you have one. I'm just going to use the generic term "pop-up" to cover all these ideas.

Merely having a pop-up will increase sign ups. It's really obvious you're asking, you've made a form that's easy to fill out, you've done everything I talked about in the basic section, but you've made it stand out. A pop-up says to your Visitor, "Here it is, do it please".

Econsultancy published a blog post a little while ago about the fact that on average, pop-ups increase a site's conversion rate of Visitor to Enquirer by 400%.

Roughly speaking, that follows what we've seen on eCommerce MasterPlan. We have a pop-up running, although I must admit it's not very well integrated or designed. It's one of the top items on my to-do list for when I've finished writing this book!

Simply by adding that pop-up to the website, we took our email sign up rate from under 1% of Visitors to a fairly steady 4%. That's a big difference, so it's well worth putting one in place.

There is a lot you can test with a pop-up, and it depends on what pop-up software you're using. There are a myriad of different options out there, and lots of great plugins.[29] Find one that works for you, have a word with your web developers and get them to put it in place.

Here are four different areas that you're going to want to test.

Placement
I mentioned this earlier when I noted I'm using "pop-up" as quite a generic term.

---

[29] If you're on WooCommerce, I recommend you take a look at Popupally. That's what I just put in place and I can't believe how much you can do with it.

Different types of pop-up placement include whole site overlays, banners that appear and sit at the top until they're filled in, or at the foot of a screen until you get rid of it or fill it in, a bit like a cookie warning.

You can have placements that are fairly small, or they can be a whole page overlay. There are lots of different formats that you can be testing, and you may want to run multiple ones at the same time.

Triggers

A lot of businesses have entry pop-ups, which you see as soon as you get to the website. You can also have pop-ups that appear as someone goes to exit your site. They can appear as Visitors scroll through, or only appear on certain pages. There are a lot of different ways to get that pop-up in front of customers, so that's a whole list of things to test.

Designs

This is a world of opportunity. Different colour buttons, texts, images, sizing... these could all make a big difference to how many sign ups you get.

Cookie Settings

If someone dismisses it, how many days before they see it again on returning to your site? That's another element you want to take a look at.

Before you get excited about these testing opportunities, find out what's possible for you and then build a testing plan around it. I love these pop-ups and they make a huge different to Visitor sign up conversions, so please do test some. It's so easy to put one or two in place on your website, but testing all the variables is probably going to take somewhere in the region of six months or more, depending on your traffic and what your technology will allow you to do.

Of course, there's the law of diminishing returns, so if you're only getting a tiny incremental increase, it's time to stop testing the pop-ups and move on to looking at incentives.

Getting email sign ups from places other than your website

How else can you encourage the email sign ups from the right customers without having to do anything on your website itself?

Twitter Adverts

On Twitter, you can now run adverts that encourage customers to sign up to your emails and enable them to do it right there.

I haven't seen any case study data on this, but I do intend on testing it myself at some point later this year when I've got the right incentive piece.

You can also do an awful lot of targeting on Twitter, to try and make sure you're in front of the right customers.

Facebook Page CTA

Many eCommerce businesses have a call to action set on their Facebook Page to "Shop with Us". That's quite a big leap in The Conversation, going straight from visiting a Facebook Page to buying. So why not test it for a month, changing that CTA over to an email sign up and taking customers through to your sign up page? See what happens to the response you're getting from that tool.

Previous Site Visitors
This is a great way to use your remarketing, targeted advertising to those who have previously visited your site.

When customers have visited the website but never bought anything, they can be identified with the Google remarketing code, the Facebook remarketing code, and pretty much any other remarketing code you're using.

The adverts sent to those customers are usually about products they looked at or others from your brand. Why not give it a go with email sign ups? Instead of a product, try something like, "Want to know more about our business? Sign up to our emails", or "Click here to find out more".

Human Interaction
This is a really important one that businesses tend to get all strange about and fail to do a lot of the time, but it's really important to make sure everyone in your team is doing it. That is simply to ask during human interactions.

If you have physical stores, make sure you're asking customers to sign up when they come in. All the above applies, apart from pop-ups (it's quite hard to do pop-ups in a physical store!). The tips I've covered apply to asking for emails when someone phones your business, emails, communicates over Facebook or customer service, and so forth. Make sure you're always asking at that point, "Would you like to be added to our email list? I think you'd find it useful, and this is what you'll get".

Competitions with Partners
If you sell fishing tackle and you have the opportunity of running a competition with Fishing Tackle Monthly, you can get free advertising space with them for offering a prize. You can also add in a sign up form, so you're both entitled to the sign up data.

This is a great way to get a large number of customers onto your list quickly from a specific partner's list.

A couple of things to remember here:

- Make sure you pick those partners carefully because you want good quality data.
- Make sure you are able to track the performance of those customers separately, so you can see if you capture good quality data from the activity.

The example below is of Cornish cookery school, Philleigh Way (philleighway.co.uk), which has teamed up with Wing of St Mawes (thecornishfishmonger.co.uk), and the magazine Cornwall Living. Wing of St Mawes and Philleigh Way put together the prize, and Cornwall Living have provided the visibility of the competition. Entry is by filling in a short questionnaire, including email address. This is a partnership that will generate awareness as well as gathering email addresses.

Win a seafood break

Enter our competition to win a seafood break in Cornwall worth £700 and a master class with Rob Wing the Cornish fishmonger

In this section, there has been a LOT of different things you can do to get more customers onto your email list, turning Visitors into Enquirers.

You cannot ever stop focusing on optimising and testing your email sign up processes. Every business is different, so never assume something will work, but if you notice something another business is doing that you think might work for you, test it!

Go back through this list again, and again, and again.

Every time you're doing a marketing planning session, look at this list and think: should you be trying to increase your email sign ups right now?

Marketing actions to turn Visitors into Enquirers

In this chapter, I've primarily been looking at the practicalities of building The Conversation and asking for the email address.

There are two marketing concepts you should also be aware of as you work on improving your Stage 2 performance.

- The impact of brand awareness.
- Using marketing to make sure customers do yo-yo back to the website if they haven't yet signed up.

You need to get any on-site improvements made before you start working on either of these. The on-site improvements alone may well lift your performance to the point where Stage 2 is no longer your worst performer or biggest opportunity.

If you've done all the on-site and Stage 2 is still the worst performer (or you've now improved all the other Stages beyond Stage 2!), it's time to tackle those two concepts.

The impact of brand awareness

The more familiar a customer is with your brand, the more likely they are to take action: visit your website, sign up to your emails, buy, buy again.

That familiarity is built with The Conversation, so the more powerful your Stage 1 Conversation is, the greater your conversion to sign up rate will be.

From a practical standpoint, this means that if your sign up rates are still not where you need them to be, it might be worth revisiting Stage 1 and starting to work on some more Shine a Light marketing. That's guest blogs, being a guest on podcasts, getting into magazines, press coverage, advertising, retail placement – there are lots of options.

Maintaining the yo-yo

The first time your Stage 1 marketing gets a customer to your website, they may well not sign up to your emails. Maybe they've not learnt enough from The Conversation to feel like it, or your call to action isn't right yet.

Various things can happen after they leave:

- You can hope that they yo-yo back again due to your on-going Stage 1 marketing.
- If they've signed up to one of your social media channels, you can increase the chances of your Stage 1 marketing working by keeping those channels active, and adding in some CTAs about your great email newsletter.

You can certainly encourage them to follow you on Twitter or Facebook, which feels like less risk for a customer and is more likely to happen early on. Maxwell Scott Bags (maxwellscottbags.com) do this on their email sign up.[30]

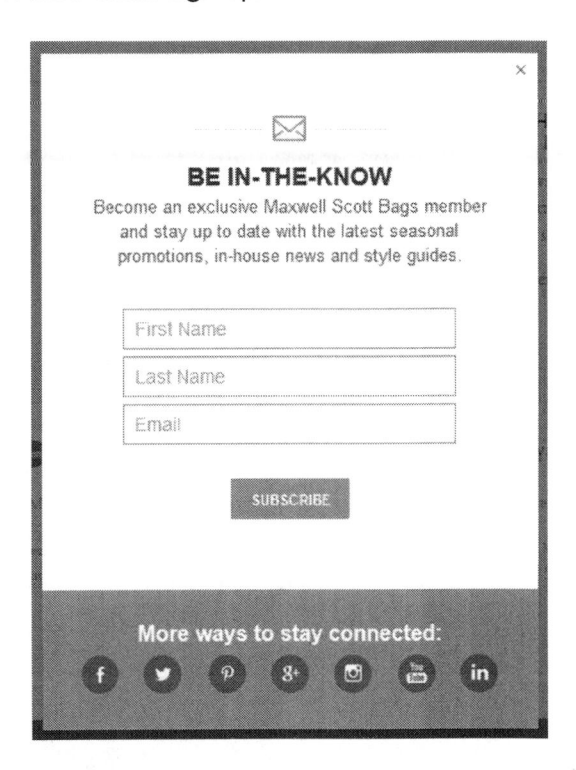

Remarketing Advertising

This is a type of marketing I don't recommend doing until:

- You have optimised everything else that you can about your pop-up.
- You have enough traffic to your site to be able to create a very accurate remarketing list that:
  - Excludes everyone who's signed up already.
  - Only includes customers who've been to your site very recently.

---

30 You can listen to my interview with Maxwell Scott Bags' Founder at eCommerceMasterPlan.com/podcast.

This can be done across a variety of platforms, with the simplest places to start being Facebook, Twitter, and Google Adwords.

The reason I don't recommend diving straight into this is because at this point, you're starting to pay for each visit. There's a lot of customers you will be marketing to, the value of each of those customers is quite low (remember the model!), and marketing budgets are generally limited – so whilst it may be very possible to get this activity to work for your business financially, there's probably somewhere better to spend the money.

If you want to test this route, start by advertising some great content (blog post, video, article) to the list, and then once they get to the site make sure they see a clear CTA to sign up. Driving them back to an email sign up is less likely to work.

Remarketing will be covered in some more detail in the coming chapters. Much more can be found at eCommerceMasterPlan.com.

Stage 2: Turning Visitors into Enquirers

Not every Visitor to your website is going to buy every time they visit, so it's really important to capture their details so you can encourage them to buy in the future.

Add pop-ups and an email address capture to provide the call to action to get those all-important sign-ups. Make sure your site is showing you to be a great business who are worthy of being given the customer's email address.

In some ways, this is the easy Stage to improve. It has the most obvious, finite list of to-dos:

- Get the right logos and trust marks on the website.
- Improve the "About Us" page.
- Get a pop-up live.

These factors might make it an easy place to start, but it's also a Stage you will never be finished with. The list of content you *could* put in to build The Conversation and get the sign up is endless; the testing and optimising you can do with your email sign up forms and pop-ups is infinite.

The great thing is that every extra sign up you get is a new opportunity to sell. And that's what I'm covering in the next Stage – how to get the first order.

6 Stage 3: Turning Enquirers into First Time Buyers

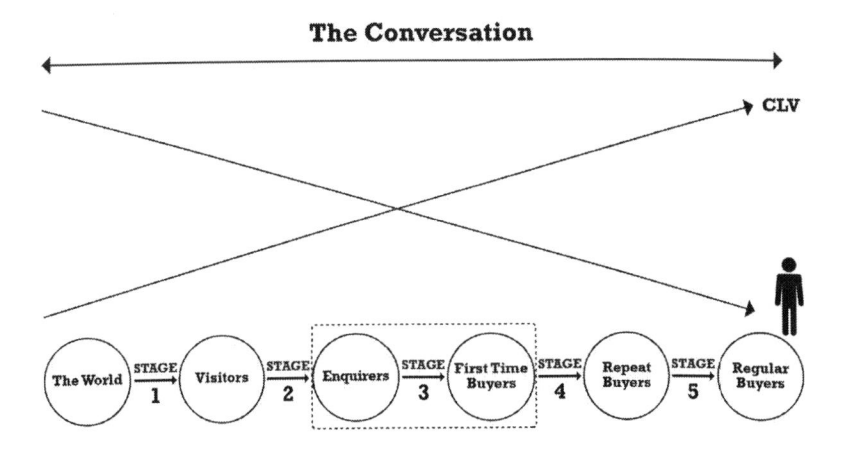

The Conversation

CLV

The World → STAGE 1 → Visitors → STAGE 2 → Enquirers → STAGE 3 → First Time Buyers → STAGE 4 → Repeat Buyers → STAGE 5 → Regular Buyers

IN STAGE 3, you finally get to think about generating the sale. The further you go through each Stage, the more your business has to lose if something goes wrong.

Customer Persuasion | 147

- You lose a great opportunity – the customer is worth more to you because they are now more likely to buy.

- You lose your investment – you've invested a lot of time, effort, and money in getting them to this Level.

- You only get so many chances – there aren't so many of these customers for you to market to.

That makes Stage 3 a really important one to invest in, to make sure you're creating as many First Time Buyers as possible.

If there are problems at this Stage, it might be because the wrong customers were brought through from the beginning of the process – so if the ideas in this chapter don't improve your performance at turning your Enquirers into Buyers, it might be because either Stage 1 or Stage 2 needs optimising to bring through a better quality of customer.

This is the first time in the model where there's only one way to get to the other side. The customer has to buy in order to get to the next Level, they can't leapfrog this Stage to become a Repeat Buyer or Regular Buyer (subscription businesses head back to Chapter 2 for an explanation on how this fits for you.

There's only one way a customer can progress any further than Stage 3. It's to make the first purchase.

At Project Repeat (projectrepeat.com), Nathan Rothstein and his team offer a service to turn people's old t-shirts into quilts and blankets. They get 8% of site Visitors signing up to email. They've targeted this because they know that getting the email address is the first step to getting the purchase. They realise that buying from them requires a lot of trust from the consumer, because they're not only going to be handling people's prized t-shirts, they're going to be cutting them up.

Immediately after someone signs up for Project Repat's 20% discount, they give them a unique code right there in the pop-up.

> Use code ████ for 20% off at checkout!
> We'll also send you an email with the coupon.
>
> Code: ████
>
> *Share The Offer with Friends!*

This is the first CTA, as well as the first opportunity for them to prove they are trustworthy – they offered 20% off, and they have delivered on that promise.

Following the sign up is the "Welcome" email, full of good messages.

- We've delivered on our promise – the 20% off code is there.
- Everyone else trusts us – "Join more than 80,000 VERY happy customers".

- You're not being overcharged – "and take advantage of the very best price for a t-shirt quilt on the internet, GUARANTEED", plus a table of price comparisons with the competition.

- We won't rush you, and we care – "P.S. You have 3 months to send in your shirts after you place your order! (but you can always ask for an extension)".

These points are then reiterated through a "Welcome Sequence", leading to 25% of their Enquirers going on to buy from them.[31]

There are now more areas of the business to consider

This is the first Stage where human interaction gets involved in The Conversation – your customer services team get on the case here.

This is also the first Stage where your products have a role to play. So from this chapter onwards, as well as marketing actions and website actions, I will discuss customer service actions and product actions.

What's the aim of Stage 3?

Stage 3 is about getting the customer to show just how much they trust your business by paying for something.

All the groundwork put in with the previous Stages should mean that by Stage 3:

- There are plenty of customers to talk to.

---

[31] You can hear my interview with Nathan at eCommerceMasterPlan.com/podcast.

- Those customers understand a fair bit about the business and feel they are in the right place.
- Those customers have already placed trust in the business by believing the marketing, visiting the website, AND providing you with their email address.

This is the Stage where all the work you've put into building The Conversation pays off.

This is the Stage where all the work you've put into bringing the right Visitors to your website pays off.

This is the Stage where all the work you've put into encouraging email sign ups pays off. Exciting!

In this chapter, I'm going to be assuming that the customer you're trying to get to buy has been through Stages 1 and 2. In real life that's not necessarily the case, but the range of marketing methods I'm discussing will also work on the customers who've taken a different route.

It also means that for this Stage to be successful, it needs to flow on from Stage 1 and Stage 2. If your Stage 3 performance is weak, it may be because your Stage 1 or Stage 2 need more work.

How does The Conversation fit into this Stage?

Through the Stages, the trust-building of The Conversation has been paying off:

- In Stage 1 you started building trust and got the customer to the website.

- In Stage 2 you built more trust and got the customer to give you their email address.

It's a big leap from visiting a website to signing up for a newsletter, and it's an even bigger leap to then buy something.

This means that, again, in Stage 3 you need to work to increase how much trust The Conversation builds.

Up until now you've been building trust in your business as a whole, and you need to continue doing that, but now you also need to build trust in your individual products. The good news is that you now have the customer's email address so you can put the messages you want them to see in front of them. At this point, you also need to prove that their trust has been well placed by treating their email address with respect.

The bad news is that not only do you need to increase the areas that The Conversation is covering, this is also the first time The Conversation leaves the control of the marketing department, as it includes human-to-human contact with another member of your wider team.

During this Stage, The Conversation needs to:

- Build trust in the products.
    - Product information
    - Customer reviews
- Continue to build trust in the business.
    - Delivery information
    - Checkout security
- Continue to deliver on the Editorial Mission.

What can my customers teach me at this Stage?

Keep paying attention to what you learnt in Stage 1 and Stage 2.

In Stage 3 you also need to start building trust in the products and promoting them to the customers you're marketing to. Your current customers can show you:

- Which products to promote.
- Which areas of customer service need improvement.
- What areas of the website need the most work to improve the flow through to the checkout.

Customer's favourite products

To get the first order, you need to put the products that the new customer is most likely to buy in front of them. Nine times out of ten, these should be your most popular products.

Looking at the analytics of what your buyers are doing can identify:

- Your best-reviewed products.
- Your top sellers.
- Your most wished for.

I'll cover how in the next section of this chapter.

Then you can shout about how much the other customers love these products in the marketing! Customers like reassurance that they're making a good buying decision, and if other customers have bought it and liked it, that's a great piece of reassurance.

Essentially if something is popular it's more attractive, because it's less of a risk to the new buyer.

Using customer service information

You can find out all sorts of things by listening in to customer service calls, and reading the emails or other communications.

- The most common questions customers ask before buying – turn these into FAQs, email newsletters, or answer them on the product's page. Make sure your customer service team are ready to answer them too.

- Which areas of the customer service mix are not up to scratch – how fast are you replying on Facebook and Twitter? Would a live chat function help? Do the customer service hours match customer requirements?

How they use the website

For this Stage, it's really important that the checkout process is as easy as possible. Any difficulties and you'll lose the order, and possibly the person, forever.

Google Analytics can be set up to provide clear stats for how well customers are progressing through your checkout. These can highlight things that might need fixing or re-thinking.

Research and prep work required

Other products to promote

What are your bestsellers in unit terms? You may already know the answer, but note that for this research it's about volume, not sales value.

Most systems will give you this information. If you have Google Analytics eCommerce Tracking fully set up, you'll find the answer under Conversions > eCommerce > Product Performance.

What are your highest reviewed products?

Most review platforms will quickly show you this. If you have lots of products scoring 5/5 or the maximum number of stars, use their sales volumes to pick between them.

You will need to revisit these lists every three to six months (or more frequently, depending on how your product mix changes) to keep your marketing up to date.

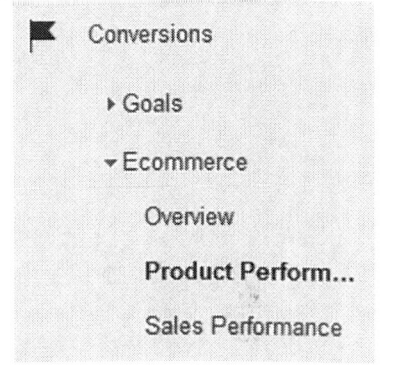

Find out what's stopping customers from completing the checkout

Once a customer has entered the checkout there's only one thing they should do, and that's finish the checkout process and buy.

Lots of customers don't do this, so you should be regularly working to find out why. A core part of that is to analyse the checkout using a funnel. The funnel will show you how many customers start the checkout process, and where they drop out.

Customer Persuasion

You can track this in Google Analytics:

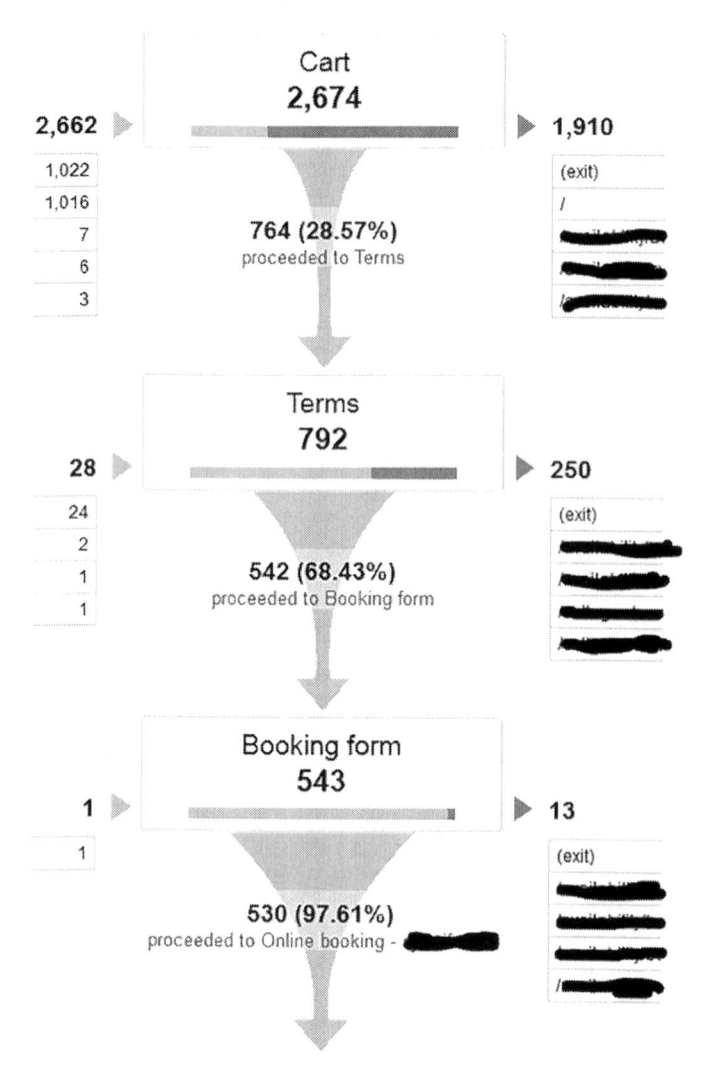

```
              Cart
              2,674
2,662  ▶  ████████░░░░░░  ▶  1,910
 1,022                        (exit)
 1,016                         /
   7        764 (28.57%)      ▬▬▬
   6      proceeded to Terms  ▬▬▬
   3                          ▬▬

              Terms
              792
  28   ▶  █████████░░░░░  ▶  250
  24                          (exit)
   2                          ▬▬▬
   1        542 (68.43%)      ▬▬▬
   1     proceeded to Booking form  ▬▬▬

           Booking form
              543
   1   ▶  █████████████░  ▶  13
   1                          (exit)
                              ▬▬▬
            530 (97.61%)      ▬▬▬
     proceeded to Online booking - ▬▬  ▬▬▬
                              /▬▬
```

In this example, the big problem is getting customers from the "Cart" to the "Terms" stages, only 28.6% of those who start the checkout process make it the "Terms" stage.

There's also a pretty big drop off between "Terms" and "Booking form" as well.

If you find any of these drop offs in your funnel, you need to investigate why customers might be exiting the checkout at that point. Look at the stage of the checkout – is it clear what to do? Are there distractions you can remove? If there's nothing obvious jumping out at you, then it will be worth getting some real life people to try it out for you.

Find out what's stopping customers from getting to the checkout

There's a lot of website to get through before a customer reaches your checkout. They have to get past the landing page, through the categories and search functionality, find a product they want, and add it to the basket.

This means it's not enough to only analyse the performance of your checkout funnel, you also need to look at how well your website is getting customers from the landing page through to the checkout.

Again you can analyse this in Google Analytics. It's a less exact science because there are so many routes the customer can take.

There are reports all ready to go in Google Analytics that can help you with this.

Behaviour Flow

This shows you the path customers are taking through the site – it's really nice and visual, and will quickly show you where customers are exiting.

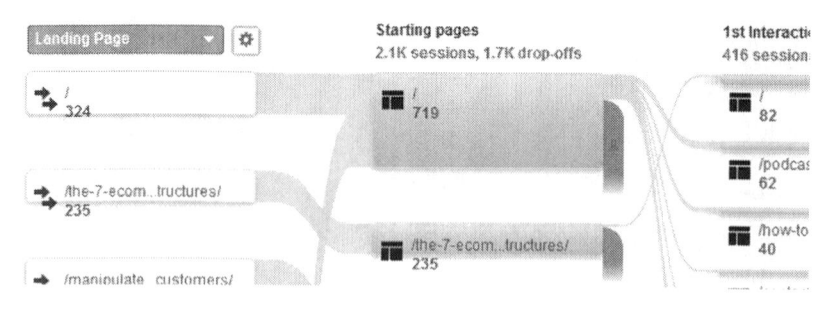

[Screenshot of Google Analytics Behaviour Flow report showing Landing Page, Starting pages (2.1K sessions, 1.7K drop-offs) and 1st Interaction (416 sessions), with flows to /, /the-7-ecom...tructures/, /manipulate customers/, /podcast, /how-to]

Once you've found those exit points, go and have a look at why customers are exiting there, and try to find a way to fix it.

Site Search Reports

If you haven't already got this set up for your website, get it done. It's pretty straightforward.

This will tell you what customers are searching for, then you can check you have the products and information they are looking for AND that your search facility is providing it to the customer.

Build Your Own Funnel

You could also build another funnel (like the checkout funnel) and use it to track how many customers make it to the category pages, and then to the product pages, to the basket, and then into the checkout.

Just like with the checkout funnel analysis, you may need to get some real life people to try it out for you...

Carry out user testing

A quick and easy way to find both the problems and the solutions is to do some user testing. This is what the big boys now rely on for every decision about their website, and many of the larger online retailers have their own in-house testing studios.

You don't need to go to those lengths of effort and cost to get some great user testing done. But also, don't just use your mum – you need to use people who are your target customer.

Sites like usertesting.com now offer a fantastic service for less than $100.

Listen to customer service for content ideas

What kind of questions are customers are asking? About the product? Delivery? Payment or returns?

If you can answer these questions or solve their problems before they need to call, you'll increase trust and the likelihood of purchase.

Either spend some time every week with the customer service team, or get them to regularly update you on common issues.

Website actions to turn Enquirers into First Time Buyers

In this chapter, I'm going to cover the website actions, customer service actions, and product actions before I dive into the marketing actions – that's because if you haven't got these bits right first, then your marketing effort is not going to be as useful. Plus, these are often quicker to get off the to-do list: it's either a quick fix, or something that should be part of your normal business routine and should never leave the to-do list!

CRO: Conversion Rate Optimisation

A lot of the research tasks I outlined above are classed as Conversion Rate Optimisation.

CRO is the process of removing the barriers to purchase on your website to make it much easier (and therefore more likely) for someone to buy. In my mind, it's not just about techy site tweaks but about the full experience of buying. In some ways, the whole of this book is about CRO!

- Bringing the right traffic to the site in the first place.
- Making content tweaks on the website to increase trust and answer questions.
- Making big content changes on the website to remove any barriers.
- Doing any techy site tweaks.

CRO is a constant process and you should never stop working on improving your site. But it's also a process that you can get lost in and achieve ever-lower returns from. Think of the law of diminishing returns, best explained to me by my A-level (high school) Economics teacher: imagine one ride-on lawn mower, mowing a football pitch. If you put two mowers on the pitch, the job gets done faster; three and it might get done faster again. But once you get to ten or more, the benefit of those extra mowers really tails off.

Make sure you don't get totally absorbed by the CRO process and forget to look up and see the bigger picture!

In this chapter, I'm not going to outline a heap of CRO tactics as what works often varies from business to business (I also covered quite a few in the last chapter).

Here are some tips for improving the checkout funnel, which work nine out of ten times.

Remove Checkout Distractions
Make sure that once a customer is in the checkout, all they can do is complete their checkout. They can't add extra items, you're not pushing them to go and buy more things, there's no email pop-up.

If you're not sure what I mean by this, take a look at the Amazon checkout.

Clear and Easy to Find Delivery Information
Delivery is consistently one of the top reasons customers don't buy from a website – they don't like the methods, the price, or they just couldn't find the information. Putting it clearly on every page and making it easy to find will improve your conversion rate. You don't want it to be the hidden spear at the end of the process, you want them to know about it up front.[32]

Mobile Checkouts
This is the checkout someone experiences when they are using a mobile version of your site. To optimise this, make sure each information entry box brings up the correct keyboard, e.g. if the customer needs to enter their phone or credit card number then bring up a numeric keypad, if they need to enter an email then bring up a keypad with an @ sign, and so forth. It's very simple to do, but many businesses don't bother.

---

32   I've written a whole book on how Delivery can help you – get hold of a copy here: eCommerceMasterPlan.com/books.

Stock Availability

The customer wants to know that their order will be completed in full, so make it clear what you have in stock. For items that are out of stock, explain when they'll be back in.

(This can also be a good time to collect email addresses – if something is out of stock, offer the customer the ability to sign up for an alert when it's back in stock.)

Don't Force Registration

Lots of checkouts try to force customers to create "an account" or a "login" before they can buy. This is a real turn-off! By all means give them the option, but don't force it.

However good your checkout is, some customers will always fail to complete it. 77% of shoppers have abandoned their shopping baskets during an online purchase:

- 61% did so because they felt delivery costs were too high.
- 29% did so because of a lack of support.
- 28% wanted to take their time to compare with other products and sites first.
- 27% came to the conclusion that the product was unsuitable for them.[33]

All of your product actions, customer services actions, and marketing actions are going to aim to reduce this number.

Using A/B split testing

Once you know the areas you think you need to improve, set up a new version of that page and test how well it does against

---

[33] "The UK Customer Service and Support Market", eDigitalResearch iAdvize report, September 2015.

the old or current version. This will make sure you're putting the right things live, and not accidentally implementing something that's not as good as the current version!

A/B split testing is the process of sending traffic to two versions of the same thing and allowing your customers to tell you which is best. There are lots of software systems available to help you do this.

Automated Merchandising or "Searchandising"

I think this is one of the most fascinating ways to improve the conversion rate of a website.

It's very clever software that analyses the activity on your website, in an attempt to present the right product to the right customer at the right time. It dynamically changes search results and product category pages in order to increase conversion.

Just like reviews software, please don't try to do this yourself – go out and buy in some best of breed software. It is a very clever science all of its own, and there is a company out there who can do what you need, much better than you can do in-house.

Product information that's not on the product pages

There's only so much information about your products that you can include on the product pages, and some information works better elsewhere. This other information often ends up on static pages or within the blog. It might include:

- The story behind each brand.

- How and why you came to pick this product.
- Product comparisons.
- Buyer's guides.

At Taste Tradition Direct (tastetradition.co.uk), they sell the crème de la crème of British meat.[34] Rare breeds, beautiful and unusual cuts, it makes your mouth water just to think about it! There are endless possibilities of content they can feature or create: recipes, information about the provenance of the product, different cuts, different breeds, the history of the different breeds, the history of butchery, the history of British meat, the people involved in the process... endless, absolutely endless, content.

Ian Smith has made a clear, focused start on content that's going to help his Visitors on the path to buying. For example, the customer might be thinking, "It's fresh meat. Will it still be fresh when it gets to me?". They need to have really clear information on the delivery system, how it's going to be parceled, when they can expect to get it, and how long it's going to be fresh for once they receive it.

The customer might also be thinking, "Golly, this is a lot more expensive than Tesco!". This is where their content about the quality of the meat comes in handy, detailing why it's worth the extra money and why this is of superb quality. That's really going to be very important.

Ian also might have to deal with the question of cooking the meat, even though it's out of his hands! Perhaps the more expensive meat is being bought for a special occasion, and the customer wants to cook it just right. Ian has made sure to cover

---

[34] You can hear my interview with Ian where we discuss this at eCommercemasterPlan.com/podcast.

this too, with blog posts about how to cook the perfect roast beef and guides on how to present a suckling pig.

The first thing you need to do is to work out what sort of content you should be putting out there and get right on with creating it.

I recommend starting off with the content you think will make the biggest difference (hint: probably a gap highlighted by the customers in your research). BUT you probably know more about the product than anyone else, so also listen to your instincts. What do you think is going to help customers buy?

This, of course, is where the gnarly question of blogging frequency comes up. There is no right answer, but if there are things your customers need to know then they should be on your blog. I get that at the start of this process there's going to be a long list of those. Start off aiming for one new post a week, or if that seems insurmountable then go for one a month.

Start chipping away at it and slowly you'll start to see the benefits coming through. Then, as you get more used to it, you'll find you can do them much, much quicker. It's little and often. Eventually you may reach the levels of Pascal Culverhouse of Electric Tobacconist (electrictobacconist.com), who spends the first two hours of every working day writing copy for his website![35]

Customer Personas

A customer persona (or "avatar") is a description of the different types of customer who might want to buy your products.

Whilst some businesses start with the different customer personas outlined from day one, for others it makes sense to create

---

35   You can find out more about Pascal's content strategy in our interview at eCommerceMasterPlan.com/podcast.

all the content for the generic buyer before identifying the personas in detail. Once you have constructed these personas, you can start to create content that appeals specifically to each different type.

To use a really basic example, the first time house buyer has very different questions and needs to the professional buy-to-let investor. Therefore, you'd need to be creating content to appeal to both of them and to help out both of them.

I'm not going to cover this in a lot of detail, but if you check out the interview with Tom Schwab of Goodbye Crutches I did with him last year, we had a great discussion about how he uses customer personas in his content creation.[36]

There is a lot you can do on the website to encourage customers to buy, make them trust you, and feel comfortable placing that first order. But many will still want some help, not just a self-service option.

Whilst I'm wrapping up the website actions here, there will be plenty of website improvements coming out of the following sections.

Product actions and product pages

Once you've reached Stage 3 in The Customer MasterPlan, you're aiming to get the customer to like the products enough to buy them. If The Conversation has been building well then you will have attracted the right customers to your website, who want the products you sell, like your business, and want to buy from it.

---

[36] You'll find it at eCommerceMasterPlan.com/podcast.

It's really important that the First Time Buyers have a good purchase experience, otherwise it's a nightmare to get them to buy again and that's where the profit really kicks in.

It all starts with which products you recommend to them as you're encouraging them to buy for the first time.

In this Stage, you need to make sure that your website is displaying:

- The products the customer wants to buy.
- The products in a way that continues The Conversation and delivers on the promises already made.
- The right information and CTAs to get the order.

Using the products themselves

The products you put in front of your Enquirers should be:

- The products you're known for, that best support The Conversation. If, like The TeaShed, you're known for selling giftable teas, don't point them towards your teapots. Point them towards your giftable teas!
- Products your customers love, either highest reviewed products or top sellers. People like to see what others like and follow the herd.
- Products that are easy to buy and receive. Focus on those that fit through the letterbox. One-size-fits-all, rather than bespoke, lower ticket price rather than your most expensive item. But still be representative of your core offering – if you sell bespoke suits, showing a customer an off-the-shelf handkerchief probably won't work.

Bonnie of Miso Tasty listened to her customers and realised that they were nervous about ordering a product they'd never tasted before. She makes it as simple and low-risk for them as possible.

168 | Customer Persuasion

- Encourages the order right from the first time they get to the website using this overlay entry pop-up (yes, pop-ups can also be used to seed the idea of purchase).

- Offers a discount to entice the first order.

10% OFF YOUR 1ST ORDER!
WHEN SIGNING UP FOR OUR NEWSLETTER!

SUBSCRIBE

- Had the free delivery message on every page.

FREE UK DELIVERY

- Offers a low price "Taster Pack" to test the product. Just £3 ($5), with free P&P!

MISO SOUP DUO 2 TASTER PACKS
£3.00

For a customer to become a First Time Buyer and find out if they like Miso Soup, they only have to risk £2.70 (£3 taster pack minus the 10% discount) and it will land on their doormat in the next couple of days. That really lowers the barriers to purchase.

There's an advert on the London Underground that's annoyed me ever since it went live, as with a few tweaks they should have been able to massively increase their conversion rate. It's an advert for Daysoft Contact lenses (daysoft.com) that states:

- £5.99 per box of 32 lenses.
- Plus 50p per box standard Royal Mail delivery.
- Minimum order 2 boxes.

They've engineered it to show the lowest possible price – £5.99 – but it's immediately apparent that there are TWO reasons why the customer must pay more. First they have to buy two boxes, and second they have to buy two lots of postage (one per box), so to get the product the customer actually has to spend £12.98.

On a one-product site, why not include P&P in the price? And why not advertise the price of two boxes, given that's what the customer has to buy?

Product information on the product pages

Customers on your website are taking a big leap when they buy from you for the first time. They're trusting that:

- You'll deliver the product they've paid for.
- The product will be as described on your website.
- The product will work and be brand new.
- The product will arrive in the agreed timescale.

The nature of eCommerce means you can't 100% resolve these fears for the customer, you just have to do everything you can to minimise the risk for them. In a physical store it's possible to deal with all of them – the customer can touch the product pre-purchase, and they are the ones responsible for making sure it gets to their home on time.

What you can do is eliminate as much uncertainty as possible, by both providing the information the customer needs to know AND continuing to build The Conversation as you do it.

The majority of this happens on the product pages. The product pages are the most important content on your website.

You've got to make sure that on each product page, you're answering all the questions the customer will ask. Unanswered questions lead to doubt, which lowers their trust in you.

For example, if you are selling shirts, your customer is going to want to know:

- Neck sizes?
- Fit?
- Colour?
- Cloth or material?
- Collar style?
- Button style?
- Cuff style?
- Cleaning requirements?
- Is it in stock?
- How quick can I get it?

All these details need to be included, usually with both text and image answers, as different customers will want the answers in different places and often things are easier to explain in one medium or the other. In the photography, you need:

- Front and back images.
- Close-up of collar.
- Close-up of buttons.
- Close-up of pockets.
- Close-up of cuffs.

In women's clothing it reaches a whole new level, with colours, sizes, style and length of tops, cut and fit of trousers... it's endless in women's clothing, even worse than shirts!

Even for simple products, there is plenty to do. If you are selling CDs, who's going to buy it if they can't see the track listing? Make sure the track listing is there, and the front and back views of the CD itself. (I realise this is a bit of an old-school example, but it makes the point clearly!)

In the world of electricals, it becomes even more complex. You've got to make sure all the codes and model numbers are there, the inputs and outputs are explained, and so on.

Think about a humble light bulb: how much information does a customer need in order to be able to buy that light bulb? Especially now there are LED and halogen options as well as the more traditional ones, all of which seem to have their own grading system, so there's a lot of information that has to be put across.

It's not just enough to pack out your product pages with all this info – you have to make it easy for the customer to digest and use and as well.

You could consider using:

- A table.
- Different tabs.
- Great images.
- A video.
- A mini infographic for the product.
- A separate article or buyer's guide on the website (see the next section in this chapter!).

Don't use the stock images that the supplier sends you. Make sure you're taking your own photography and that you're putting it in the style of your brand.

After all these details, don't forget the emotive sales copy on the page. It should make the customer want the product and continue The Conversation.

Each product type has its own list of things that need to be on the product page, so focus on adding the ones that will be the most helpful for your customer because that will increase sales the fastest.

To get started with the products:

1. First identify your top 10% bestselling products in terms of units (not sales value).
2. Work through those and get them right.
3. Take what you've learnt getting this top 10% right and turn it into a guide for how to add any new product, so as they go live, your new products will be done right first time.

4. Then work through the rest of the live products, tackling them 10% at a time (if there are products that are discontinued and in the sale, feel free to skip them, unless you're struggling to shift the product).

If you follow this method then the task will feel less overwhelming and you'll be getting the biggest impact the fastest.

CGC and social proof

As well as building the trust that will lead to the purchase by answering customer's questions and keeping the consistency of The Conversation, you can also make specific changes to the product pages to increase that feeling of trust.

As I've mentioned a number of times, seeing someone else trust you can make a big difference to how much a new customer will trust you. There are lots of ways you can add proof that others trust you to your product pages. These types of content are referred to as "social proof", and are another type of Customer Generated Content (CGC), like reviews and awards.

All those trust marks I discussed in Chapter 5 can be used on the product page, but you can do more than this.

The most obvious way is to ask your customers to review each product they buy. I strongly recommend integrating a reviews solution, not just using the one that comes with the website system you bought. Having review functionality on a website is easy; getting customers to review is very hard! And the bigger you get, the more difficult it becomes to manage the reviews. Proper review software will solve those problems for you, and it also adds another layer of trust because the customer will see you're using a recognised provider of reviews. Some of the companies that my podcast guests are using to manage their reviews include Yopto, Feefo, Trustpilot, and Bazaarvoice.

Once you've got reviews coming in, you have two great ways to increase trust on the product page.

1. The combined stars from the reviews – these should be somewhere near the top of the page.

2. The reviews themselves, which should be easy to see and access on the page.

Another very cool (and much less widely used) way to get this social proof onto the product page is via real-time updates.

These often also create an urgency for the purchase. The travel broker websites are particularly good at doing this.

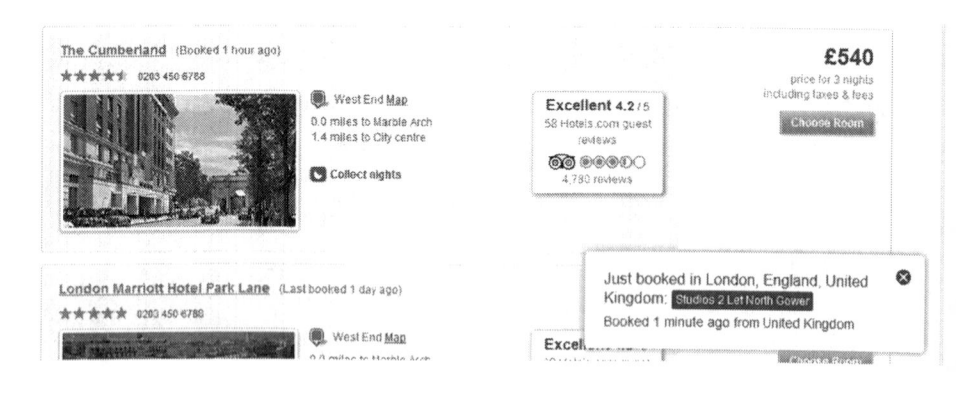

This yellow pop up box on hotels.com tells the customer that someone booked something in the area they're looking at, within the last minute. This builds trust because it shows that the site is actively trading, and other customers are using it (right now!). It also creates a sense of urgency – "I'd better buy now or I might miss out". Urgency and scarcity are always effective in increasing orders.

Stage 3: Turning Enquirers into First Time Buyers | 175

The "(Booked 1 hour ago)" next to the hotel name also increases the feeling of urgency to get the booking. This statement makes the customer more likely to choose The Cumberland than London Marriott Hotel Park Lane because The Cumberland appears to be more popular – it's been booked more recently.

Note also how they're using their own customers' ratings AND those from Trip Advisor to help customers find the right hotel for them. Reviews are very powerful.

If you want to take this to another level, take a look at what Very.co.uk are doing. It's social proof as a CTA, taken to the max!

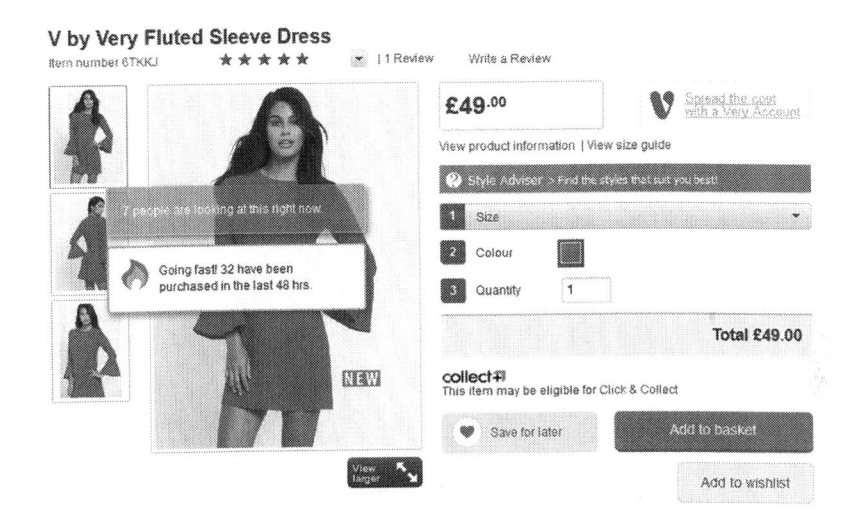

The two boxes pop-up over the image as you're looking and various messages might be shown. All of them are about how much the other customers are interested.

- "X people are looking at this right now."
- "Going fast! 32 have been purchased in the last 48 hrs."

- "Purchased 23 times in the last 24 hours."
- "Purchased 21 times in the last 48 hours."

They each focus on a mix of urgency, scarcity and popularity.

Customer service actions to turn Enquirers into First Time Buyers

In this Stage, it's highly likely that some of your Enquirers will end up having a one-to-one conversation with your customer services team. That might be via:

- A live chat box on the website.
- Instant message conversation – some businesses are now using WhatsApp and text messages for customer services.
- A live conversation – phone call, Facetime, Skype.
- Email.
- Social media – either public posts or private messaging.

You don't get to choose the methods. You need to be available and servicing your customers via the systems they want to use. You also don't get to choose when your customer service hours are, as that's based on when your customers want to be served.

It's also in your interests to respond FAST – that's within minutes or seconds, never within days. If a customer wants an answer they probably want it now, especially if it's during their first purchase decision. If you don't get back to them quickly enough on email, they'll contact you on Facebook, then on Twitter, then on live chat, then they'll phone, creating a lot more work for your team and a very annoyed customer. After that sort of experience they're going to trust you less, making an order harder to get.

Recent UK research found that these are the criteria customers see as the most important for online customer service:

- 68% of customers want a quick response.
- 56% want to be able to make contact for free.
- 46% expect to be able to contact an agent instantly.
- 25% would like to have one person handling their order.
- 23% want a friendly agent.
- 21% want to be able to contact in extended hours.
- 18% want to contact someone who has access to their history.
- 12% want to be able to easily locate the contact information.[37]

It really is all about ease and speed.

Expectations of speed vary by support channel.

- **Social media:** 1/3 expect a reply within 30 minutes.
- **Email:** 39% expect an answer within 2 hours.
- **Phone:** 35% expect an answer within 1 minute, and 66% within 5 minutes.
- **Web Call Back:** 21% expect an answer within 1 minute.
- **Live Chat:** 17% expect an answer within 30 seconds, 48% expect an answer within 1 minute.[38]

---

37 "The UK Customer Service and Support Market", eDigitalResearch iAdvize report, September 2015.

38 "The UK Customer Service and Support Market", eDigitalResearch iAdvize report, September 2015.

And the majority of people (64%) would buy more if real-time support was available.

The customer service systems

Please don't think you need to turn all possible customer service channels on 24/7 by next week.

As well as proving great customer service, you also have to make a profit, so focus on the changes that will make the biggest impact on customers for the right price first. And test everything.

Start by working out the practicalities. Which ones can you cover well enough right now, and which will have to be future projects? Ask yourself:

- Which customer service channels you should be providing and using.
- When your customer service should be manned.
- How you are going to implement this. Outsourcing? Staggered working hours? Bonuses per sale for anyone who works evenings?

I suggest you run some tests of the impact of being open longer before you change everyone's contract!

Customer service training

Before turning on a pile of new customer service systems, make sure your team are delivering a great service consistently.

As I was working on this book, one of my Facebook friends posted the following to my newsfeed. It's a great example of why consistent training is really important.[39]

> Interesting experience I just had with 1and1 customer service (and perhaps a customer service lesson in here)
>
> Call their customer service number. Get rep #1. Explain that I screwed up and missed the email notifying me of a rebill and ask if they can reverse that, refund me, and cancel that account. Rep immediately says, "No, we can't do that. We sent you an email." I reply, "Yes, I understand I received an email, and completely take full responsibility, but I'm asking for your help to please reverse that. I have about 30 other domains with you, but I don't use this particular account anymore, so I'd like to cancel that domain and the hosting with it."
>
> He asks for some information and looks at my account.
>
> **Rep #1:** "So to confirm, you'd like me to cancel that domain?"
>
> **Me:** "Yes, please -- as well as the hosting that goes with that particular domain."
>
> **Rep #1** (annoyed sounding): "Ok, wait, so you would like to cancel your hosting with us as well?"
>
> **Me:** "I would like to cancel the hosting associated with that particular domain, not ALL of my hosting with you."
>
> **Rep #1:** "... so you would like to cancel your hosting with us?"
>
> **Me** (now very annoyed): "Yes, please."

---

39   Isn't it great when examples you need just pop up when you need them! A big thank you to Tim Paige of Lead Pages for letting me use this in the book:
www.thevoiceoftimpaige.com and www.leadpages.net.

> **Rep #1:** "Let me transfer you."
>
> About 60 seconds later, Rep #2 gets on the line, says it looks like I was transferred but Rep #1 hasn't finished notating the account yet, so asks how he can help. I explain the situation, apologize for the error on my part, and ask politely for his help.
>
> **Rep #2:** "Oh absolutely! Happens all the time, I can get this refunded for you and cancel that account. I also see you have two different domains that look like they lead to the same place, would you like them both cancelled as well to avoid future charges?"
>
> WOW! Now that's customer service. Here's hoping Rep #1 was just having a bad day, because under other circumstances, I might have been moving EVERYTHING to another registrar. Rep #2 saved my business by refunding one tiny charge. Was it worth it for them to keep $1,000's of my business to refund $83?

The customer service team needs training in the technicalities of the new methods, but more importantly about how everything they do fits into The Conversation.

You're going to need to make sure your customer services team understand:

- The theory of The Conversation – why it's important and its impact.
- Your business's Conversation and Editorial Mission Statement.
    - What are the key messages to put out there?
    - What is being done to improve things further?
    - Show them what marketing is live.
    - Explain who the customers you're bringing to the website are.

But it's not just about training them in The Conversation. You also need to put the systems in place to enable them to do their part in building The Conversation.

I recently needed to claim under a guarantee for an electrical item that stopped working. I'd lost all the paperwork, but the company concerned were great at sorting that out, confirming they would be able to pick up the item and deliver it back to me fixed a week later. (They also did a great job of selling me an upgrade at the same time – so my item would be back, working, and better within in about two weeks!)

After that it all became a bit of a nightmare, particularly annoying as I know this business shouts about how it really cares about creating great experiences for its customers.

Before anything could be booked in, I had to pay for the upgrade – but I had to do that over the phone and their phone lines are only open during business hours (which really doesn't work for me – if it's work time, I'm working). There were only a handful of reps who were able to process my order, and in fact one of the times I called up I was on hold so long I bounced back to a very confused receptionist.

Then it turns out they hadn't put through the payment then and there (as I'd requested) so the whole call-us-to-pay saga started again when the card details wouldn't go through, which in turn delayed both pick up and return. In all, it took over a month for me to have the item working and back with me.

To be fair to the team, they tried their hardest, but the systems just weren't set up to help them.

Here's a few simple things that could have been done to make it easier for everyone:

- A custom order electronic payment link – you can do it with a normal PayPal account so it doesn't have to be complex.
- Longer customer service hours.
- An online repair booking service.

If one of those were in place, the whole thing could have been achieved within a much shorter time span. This would have saved the business time and money, and returned my product much faster.

You need to make sure your team have the training, resources, and systems in place to be able to deliver on the promise you've been making customers during The Conversation.

Marketing actions to turn Enquirers into First Time Buyers

Once the basics are sorted for turning Enquirers into First Time Buyers, you can get on with actively encouraging them to make that purchase.

But don't think you can forget the trust-building Conversation at this point – it still has to be part of everything you're putting in front of customers.

I'm going to focus mainly on email marketing here because it's the strongest way to turn an Enquirer into a First Time Buyer. Andy Mulcahy, Editor at IMRG in the UK, said: "In recent years we've actually seen the percentage of revenue derived from email marketing (vs. other forms of marketing) increase sharply – rising from 7.7% in 2010 to 13.9% in 2014". It's working for everyone else, so make it work for you with these simple sequences.

Using a Welcome Sequence

This is the most important piece of marketing for turning an Enquirer into a First Time Buyer.

It's important because:

- It's very powerful for quickly driving a response.
- The customer has just trusted you with their email address, and you want to prove you are worthy of that trust fast – which is the job of the welcome email!
- It's a great way to get the right messages for The Conversation in front of these Enquirers.

You may remember the Project Repat example in the last chapter – well, it's their Welcome Sequence that enables Nathan to turn 25% of his Enquirers into Buyers.

A "Welcome Sequence" is a series of communications that you send to someone after they've given you their email address. Usually these are emails, but it can include other communication methods too if they fit. Here I'm going to focus purely on the email method, but the same theories hold if you're adding in other methods like SMS or post.

The role of the Sequence is to:

- Continue The Conversation and build further trust with the customer.
- Get them to buy, fast.

- Do some clever email stuff to improve the chances of you ending up in the inbox (email deliverability).
- Make good on whatever promise you made as they signed up (great content? 10% off?).

Let's get that clever deliverability stuff out of the way.

Each email system (Gmail, Outlook, Hotmail) has its own algorithm for deciding what to do with each email it receives. Should it go into the inbox? Should it go into spam? Should it just not get delivered at all? There are lots of different ways to improve your chances of reaching the inbox, and the art of doing that is referred to as "email deliverability". Some email deliverability relies on the recipients of your emails actively doing something – and that's the area you're interested in for the Welcome Sequences.

During the Welcome Sequence (and all the emails!) you want customers to interact – open them, click on them, and reply to them. In the Welcome Sequence, you also want them to add you to their safe senders or whitelist.

The sooner someone starts doing all these things with your emails, the better. So in your very first email you should:

- Ask them to add your business to their safe senders.
- Give them a reason to reply.
  - "Help us out, Tell us what your favourite X is."
  - "We're running a competition to win Y – just reply to enter."
- Give them lots of reasons to click on the email.
  - "Click here to redeem your sign up offer."
  - "Here's our bestseller."
  - "Click here to fill in a little survey so we can send you better emails."

- "Click here to give us your postal address so we can send you a free car sticker (bumper sticker, US friends!)."
- "Click here to follow us on Facebook/Twitter/Instagram."
• AND of course, give them whatever you've promised!
  - If it was a promotional offer, explain how to redeem it.
  - If it was "great content" then confirm that's going to happen.

And that pretty much takes care of the first email!

Needless to say, it should be delivered within minutes of them signing up. For the subsequent emails, I'd suggest you send one a day for the first three to four days, then slow it down to one a week or so (but don't forget to test).

There are two particularly great things about a Welcome Sequence:

1. You can build it email by email, put it live as soon as you have the first email ready, then just bolt on each extra email as you create them.

2. It's automated, which means once you set it up it runs forever. Whatever email system you use (whether it's as simple as MailChimp, or as powerful as dotmailer), it should be possible set up a series of emails that automatically flow out each time someone signs up.

What should the emails from number two onwards be about?

They should be a mixture of CTAs to buy, and content that builds The Conversation.

For example:

1. The welcome email as outlined above; focused on The Conversation
2. Our top 5 highest rated products/ top 5 bestsellers; focused on CTA to buy
3. Our story; focused on The Conversation
4. What makes it really easy to buy from us; focused on CTA to buy/ The Conversation
5. Our team; focused on The Conversation
6. The best products to get started with; focused on CTA to buy
7. What makes our products so great; focused on The Conversation / CTA to buy

You'll see that although there are several really big CTAs in here, each of them supports your Conversation's aim to increase trust.

The first one to put out there is about the highest rated products or best sellers. This is using the Welcome Sequence to illustrate:

- That your existing customers love and trust you, so they can too.
- What everyone else is buying, which makes their decision easier.

The one about "how to buy from us" will be different for each business, but you should head-on tackle what you've learnt from your customers about the barriers to purchase. From the feedback your customers have given you, you might need to:

- Explain delivery options.
- Explain how to choose the right size.

- Explain the returns process.
- Explain different payment options.

If you have a complicated product set – furniture, or mattresses, or bespoke products – you may want to send several of these, one on each different topic.

"The best products to get started with" is more advice on how to get started with sampling or trying out your business – for Bonnie from Miso Tasty, this would be a great time to do a whole email featuring the £3 sample pack.

The order of the emails will change from business to business. You should put the one that will help the most with The Conversation first, and try to alternate the buying messages with trust-building messages.

Once someone finishes the Welcome Sequence, they should then be moved into your normal broadcasts system.

If you want some companies who are great at Welcome Sequences, go to: eCommerceMasterPlan.com/welcome-sequences for my regularly updated list.

The Welcome Sequence is very much the key piece of marketing here. Once you have that sorted out and you want to take Stage 3 up a notch, here are a couple of further ideas.

Using Abandoned Basket reminders

However good your checkout is, customers will fail to complete it.

That's because life gets in the way! Maybe the tablet runs out of battery, the microwave pings, or you can't remember your exact shoe size in that particular brand.

In Q4 2015, the average retail business saw 72.2% of baskets abandoned, increasing to 84.4% in the travel sector.[40]

As an eCommerce business, you can't stop these things from happening. Instead, you need to find ways to make sure the customer comes back and finishes off their purchase. One way to do that is to set up "abandoned basket" reminders.

These are usually emails, but can also be text messages, sent out after someone abandons their basket before checking out on your website.

Not sure if you should invest in this? Research by SaleCycle back in 2013 showed that the AOV of an abandoned basket customer is 18.8% higher than typical purchases (which suggests they come back and add another item). and the average abandoned basket email sent delivers $6 in revenue.

More recent data from SaleCycle (from Q4 2015) has abandoned basket emails achieving a 40% open rate, a 27% click through rate, and the conversion rate from a click to your website from an abandoned basket email is, on average, 27% (that's twenty-seven percent – it's not a typo).

There are some simple rules to follow to make these reminders as successful as possible, and how much of this you can do depends on how much of this information you can integrate into your emails.

Rule 1: Speed
You need to send it fast, ideally within the first hour.

---

40   Q4 Remarketing Report", SaleCycle.com, 2015.

The faster you send it, the greater the conversion rate. SaleCycle found that if you send a reminder within 28 minutes of the basket being abandoned, then the conversion rate is 5.3%. But if you leave it over an hour, then that rate drops to 3.6%. Leave it until the next day and it's just 2.6% (so still worth doing if that's all your systems can cope with).

Rule 2: Subject Line
Always use a good, relevant subject line. Include detail.

"You left your basket behind" is OK, but you can do better. Include clear, specific details so the customer knows exactly what's happening.

- Your company name.
- Details of the products.
- A tone of urgency.
- Make it seem like it's coming from customer services not marketing.

You're going to need to do some testing to get it right for you, but try all of this and it could get the open rate over 50%!

Rule 3: More Detail
Make sure that the email is useful, and include detail (again). Put in as much about the abandoned basket as you can get your systems to deliver, specifically product names, prices, and images.

Open with a customer service style paragraph, with text links back to the basket and a sense of urgency, then end that paragraph with a clear "Complete your Order" button.

Follow with a basket recreation and another "Complete your Order" button.

Rule 4: Test

Once you've got the above working, use it as a simple benchmark to test what works for you.

- Try adding a second communication a day later, repeating the message to those who still haven't checked out (if that works, try adding a third!).

- What impact does an offer make? Try free P&P or 10% off. Be careful with this one, or you may find that customers remember abandoning and waiting will get them a discount.

I've pinned several useful infographics about this on The Customer MasterPlan Pinterest board, which you'll find here: uk.pinterest.com/ChloeThomasECMP.

For Turtle Mat (previously mentioned in Chapter 2) getting the first order is really important because it's unlikely they'll get a repeat purchase. Here's the abandoned basket email they use to increase how many Enquirers they turn into First Time Buyers. It's triggered 45 minutes after the basket is abandoned, and the subject line is "Can we help you with your order?".

CAN WE HELP YOU WITH YOUR ORDER?

We noticed that you've added some products to your shopping basket but left without completing your order. We've saved these items for you so you don't miss out, but don't forget to come back soon as our most popular and limited edition mats may sell out! You can also complete your order now by clicking the link below.

If you have questions about placing your order online our customer service team are happy to help, you can contact them on **0345 600 3478**.

COMPLETE YOUR ORDER

	Qty	Price
Chrysanthemum	1	£49.95
	Total:	£54.90

COMPLETE YOUR ORDER

The main part of the email includes a lot of the details I've been discussing, then they have added this great message into the footer:

Not sure you've made the right choice?

Why not take a look at our best selling designs

Shop best sellers

Just like the Welcome Sequence, you can start with one email and add further messages as you need to.

CRM-based remarketing

This is quite a new form of remarketing, and one that not everyone is yet familiar with.

It involves adding a list of email addresses, phone numbers, or sometimes other data, into a remarketing platform, and then marketing to those customers via the platform.

This is most commonly being done on Facebook at the moment. Facebook takes the list and tries to find those customers on their platform, then puts them into a list that you can target your marketing at.

Some email systems can integrate with Facebook ads so that your list is constantly up to date. If you can't do that, then a weekly or monthly update is probably fine depending on what messages you're giving them, e.g. if all of your ads say "place your first order" then putting them in front of customers who have already bought will erode trust, but if all of your ads say "buy now" it's OK to target everyone.

To use this to turn your Enquirers into First Time Buyers, take the list of those who have enquired but never bought and load them up, then put marketing in front of them that encourages a purchase. This might be ads of your best-reviewed products, best sellers, or starter packs, or sponsored posts about how to buy.

Essentially the same messages as you're putting out in the Welcome Sequence!

Cookie-based remarketing

If you have enough traffic going through your website, you can also use normal cookie-based remarketing to market to the Enquirers.

Use similar messages to the Welcome Sequence again, but this time target those who have landed on the email sign up confirmation page and not on the "order placed" page.

With Google you might also want to test using RLSA (Remarketing Lists for Search Advertising) to bid up on certain keywords for these customers.

Dynamic remarketing

This is usually done on Google, and enables Google to put products that someone has looked at in front of them as they go around the web. This is a great way to encourage that first purchase, because the customer will be reminded of the exact products they were looking at and be encouraged back to your website to buy.

A warning about promotions

Think very carefully about whether you want to offer a discount or a free P&P offer to get the first order.

Whilst it is highly likely it will have a positive impact on conversion, you run the risk of creating a list of customers who only ever respond to offers.

I always advocate starting with a no-offer position, using that to understand the natural response to these methods, then testing promotions after that benchmark is set to see whether it's worth any uplift it creates.

Any promotion you run should get the customer to do what you want them to do as cheaply as possible.

Stage 3: Turning Enquirers into First Time Buyers

There's a huge amount you can do to turn as many of your Enquirers (and Visitors) into First Time Buyers. From improving your website, to encouraging them to buy, to making sure that once they've decided to buy they actually do it.

This is a complicated Stage in The Customer MasterPlan, but the good thing is that if you get these actions right, it will also help to get Repeat Buyers and Regular Buyers. So all the effort you spend working on Stage 3 should just keep on paying back.

This is the Stage where the great majority of the results of your efforts can be tracked and measured. This should mean it's easy to make sure the effort you're putting in is the right effort – the time, money and energy that will make the biggest difference to your sales.

Always make sure you're looking at the performance of what you're doing in this Stage every month, and quickly deal with any drop offs in performance.

This is a Stage that many businesses either neglect or pay lip service to, so if you can get this right you'll be ahead of the pack.

7 Stage 4: Creating Repeat Buyers

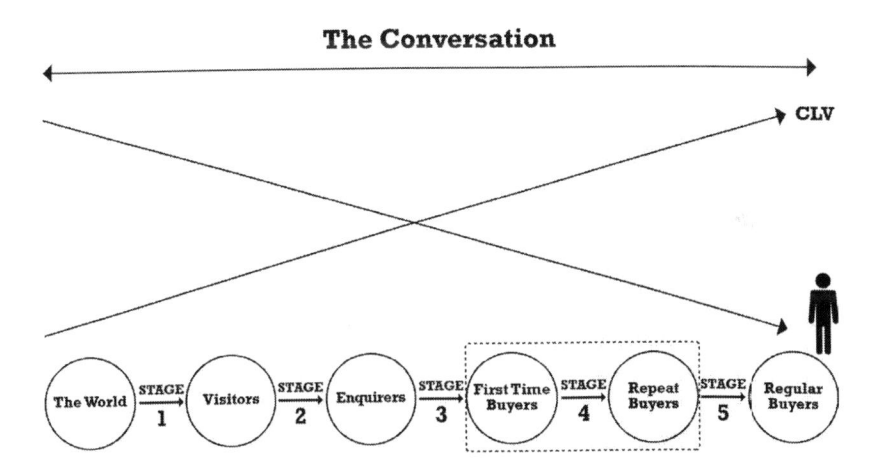

The Conversation

CLV

The World — STAGE 1 → Visitors — STAGE 2 → Enquirers — STAGE 3 → First Time Buyers — STAGE 4 → Repeat Buyers — STAGE 5 → Regular Buyers

THIS IS the Stage where you should start to make a profit.

In Stage 3, the customer did start to give your business money, but it probably wasn't enough to cover the cost of the product as well as all the marketing and effort that went into getting that first purchase. If you're recruiting new buyers at break-even, then you're doing pretty well.

That means to make the business more profitable, you need to make sure you're actively encouraging customers to buy again (and again, and again, and again) because that's where the profit starts to build up.

There are some key marketing methods to put in place, but a lot also depends on customer service, and the delivery of the goods.

> Tom Schwab of Goodbye Crutches (goodbyecrutches.com) sells alternatives to crutches for people who've recently broken a limb.[41] You might think that there's very little opportunity for them to create Repeat Buyers (let's face it – morally Tom and his team don't want to hear from their customers again because it would mean they've broken another limb!). However, it's often the case that the first purchase is to test out the alternative, and then the customer will come back for a second item or another solution.
>
> Tom recognised this opportunity and set about building a post-purchase nurture sequence to encourage a second purchase. It includes information on how to use the product they've purchased, tips on how to deal with other issues that can come along as a result of a break (e.g. depression), and, of course, a certain amount of upselling.

---

41   Hear more about how Tom does this in our podcast interview, which you can find at eCommerceMasterPlan.com/podcast.

What's the aim of Stage 4?

In Stage 4, you want to get your First Time Buyers to buy again and become Repeat Buyers.

Not only is a First Time Buyer usually an unprofitable customer, unless you do something to get them to come back, they might not buy from you again.

Just like the email sign up being a way for the customer to see if it's worth putting their trust in you, the first purchase is the next test – do you deliver on your promises when there is money at stake? Do you care about your buyers?

The First Time Buyer is someone who has not yet bought into your business's message, brand, and products. Think about how you've been using The Conversation to get the customer to trust your business. You got them to trust you enough to give you their email address, then you got them to trust you enough to place an order, but they are still testing you out and looking to see if you are worthy of their trust. They are not yet a diehard fan.

You've done a lot of work to get them to test you out, so this Stage is about proving to as many of them as possible that you are trustworthy and able to provide what they need.

The order process (placing the order, the delivery, the customer service communications, and the product itself) will be enough to convince some that you are a business they want to do more with. But for many of your First Time Buyers, you're going to need to work a bit harder to convince them.

You may think that's easy, and not something you need to put any effort into – well, that would be wrong!

- Only 5% of customers (those who've already purchased from you once) will return to your site.
- Only 3% will make another purchase.[42]

As you know from the RFM model I discussed back in Chapter 2, it's really important to get things happening quickly. Recency is very powerful. There's a lot that can be done in this Stage to encourage the second purchase to be made faster.

Once you have their second order:

- Their potential value to the business soars.
- The chances of them ordering again goes up a great deal.
- The order should have been profitable.

This Stage is also laying the foundations to turn someone into a Regular Buyer – one who comes back, again and again, to buy from you.

By this point, all the necessary research has been done and there are also no website actions in this chapter. Everything in the last chapter about improving your website will help turn First Time Buyers into Repeat Buyers, just like it helps turn Enquirers into First Time Buyers.

As you improve each Stage of your Customer MasterPlan you'll be getting more and better quality traffic coming through your site, which means you'll be able to do more useful CRO research.

---

42   Bronto research

Make sure you keep looking into it and checking for areas from the previous Stages that might be worthwhile to improve.

How does The Conversation fit into this Stage?

Again, you need to build on The Conversation you've already started and deliver on all those promises – this is not the time to drop the ball!

By this point, the customer has tested your business on every front and experienced pretty much every area of it. The primary focus has now switched from "this is who we are, believe in us", to "you were right to trust us, aren't we just what you've been looking for".

It's more about what you do (and how you do it) than what you say you're going to do.

This goes back to creating an emotion with your customers. Remember the quote from Maya Angelou?

> *"I've learned that people will forget what you said, people will forget what you did, but people will never forget how you made them feel."*

Remember the research you've already done (see Chapters 3 and 4) to make sure you know what your customers want from you, and make sure you're delivering on that in this Stage so they feel great about your business.

That's the job of The Conversation in this Stage: to make sure every part of your business is in sync and delivering on the promises you've made.

What can my customers teach me about what I should be doing at this Stage?

In this Stage, you're trying to turn customers into better customers. So there's plenty that can be learnt from your existing customers!

Second order products

What do your customers usually buy after their first testing-you-out order?

Going back to the Miso Tasty case study from the last chapter, after the customer has tried the taster pack and enjoyed it, what is the next thing they usually go on to buy? If Bonnie simply excludes the taster packs from her best sellers analysis she'll quickly see which product to market to get the second order.

If you don't have much of a product difference between the first and subsequent orders, then focus on those best sellers again, just like you did in the last Stage.

The identified items should be front and centre of your marketing to get the First Time Buyers to buy again.

Repeat purchase behaviour

How quickly do customers buy again? What's the average time between orders for your customers?

This will give you an idea of when the bulk of your post-purchase marketing needs to be done. For most businesses there will be a window straight after the first order – they were testing you out after all!

There are other ways to think about repeat purchases. For example, if you sell a pack of 60 multivitamins with instructions to take one a day, the need for a repeat purchase should arise 60 days after the last order.

Depending on your industry sector, the average time between orders might not be the right metric to look at. If you are in the gift industry, it might make more sense to consider seasons.

If you sell holidays, there are two times when someone is most likely to book again: at the same time of year as they last booked with you (January bookers book in January), or straight after they get back from the holiday they've just been on.

So what's the sweet spot, the key window in which you need to be marketing to get the next order? Think this through and factor those timelines into when your marketing happens.

Existing marketing activity performance

In Chapter 4 I looked at a lot of ways to research which marketing methods you should keep using, and which you should be testing. For this Stage you should revisit that research, and consider which of the outcomes would be useful for getting a customer to buy for the second time.

Often it will be a marketing method you're already using, but you'll be tweaking the targeting or the message to make it fit the First Time Buyer audience better.

There's a lot of marketing methods that can be done at this point, so make sure you've done the research to work out which ones you should focus on. It's also great to start by tweaking your existing marketing before launching anything new because this tends to give you faster results.

Customer service actions to turn a First Time Buyer into a Repeat Buyer

The most important thing to do at this Stage is to keep on top of everything. Don't drop the ball!

Your customer service team need to be doing everything I discussed in the last chapter, as well as delivering a great order. But in this Stage getting the customer service right is about more than just your customer service team. It's also about the delivery.

The parcel

The delivery itself needs to go well, as this is the ultimate proof that the customer placed their trust in the right business.[43] So make sure:

- Your delivery method (couriers, digital, postal, lockers, click and collect) lives up to everything that's been promised. Not just the speed but everything The Conversation has conveyed.

- Delivery information is accurately and simply conveyed to the customer.

- The basic expectations are met. The parcel arrives in good condition, and the products arrive in perfect condition with all the right paperwork.

---

[43] To find out more about how your Delivery Strategy can increase repeat purchases, get hold of a copy of my book, *eCommerce Delivery: How your Delivery Strategy Can Increase Your Sales* at eCommerceMasterPlan.com/books.

- All the expectations are met. The parcel lives up to everything that's been promised. Not just the speed but also the rest of The Conversation

If something goes wrong...

Fix It fast, and well.

Whilst no one wants an upset customer, it's a great opportunity to prove just how much you care. A customer with a problem who's well-served can quickly become a customer for life. At Tanya Heath Paris, (tanyaheath.com), a designer shoe brand) they have identified that all ten of their best customers experienced a problem early in their relationship that the customer service team did a great job of fixing.[44] It's well worth solving customers problems!

Make sure your team have the training to fix things and the flexibility to do so quickly, without having to jump through a lot of hoops to keep your customers happy.

This customer service actions section might only be short, but it's vitally important to the success of this Stage, so don't assume just because there aren't many words that there is not a lot to do.

Product actions to turn a First Time Buyer into a Repeat Buyer

Before I dive into the marketing you're going to use to increase the number of First Time Buyers who buy again, and tips to

---

44 Hear me discuss this with Tanya herself in our interview at eCommerceMasterPlan.com/podcast.

speed up that process, I wanted to mention the important role of your products.

Whilst this book is primarily about the marketing you need to do to move customers along in the journey, your products have a key role to play.

They must fit with what you're talking about in The Conversation, and be what the customer wants. Most of this was covered in Stage 3, but there are a few more points that become pertinent in Stage 4.

Product selection

You need to have the products that your customers want to buy, and expand your range in the right direction.

Think very carefully about what should be in your range, and where the depth should be. If you sell tea should you also sell teapots? How many flavours is the right number of flavours?

There also needs to be products for them to progress onto. This might be:

- A good, better, best comparison.
- Matching or complementary items.

Product quality

Not only do you need to pick the right products in the first place, you also need to monitor the quality of them before you send them out to your customer.

It might not be your fault if the supplier sends you a dodgy batch, but it is your fault if you leave it for the customer to discover the problem and don't fix it first.

Marketing actions to turn a First Time Buyer into a Repeat Buyer

Much of the marketing I've talked about in previous Stages will have an impact on the First Time Buyers too – it all builds up.

There are some key marketing methods you should be using to encourage the second purchase, and get it to happen faster.

Using direct communication campaigns

These might include email, SMS, and post. Anything that is addressed directly to the customer themselves and which lands in their "inbox" – be that on their phone, email, or doormat – is part of your direct communication campaign.

These regular communications will go out to every customer you have the details of and the right to contact. They should be focused on getting a sale and building The Conversation, and are absolutely key to getting that second purchase.

Using a Post Purchase Sequence

The first purchase was to test you out, so there's a strong chance of getting the second order very quickly as they should now trust you enough to place a bigger order.

That means you need to follow up fast to get that next order in. (All these tactics should work on any buyer, so if you can't split out First Time Buyers from Repeat Buyers don't worry about it – just put these tactics live, and replace "your second order" with "your next order".)

The Post Purchase Sequence should start AFTER they have received the first order – that's the point at which they get confirmation they were right to trust you in the first place.

The Post Purchase Sequence is all about telling them to order again.

It may or may not be encouraged with an offer or discount. As ever, start without one then test the incentive. Any incentive at this Stage should:

- Be time bound – "Free Delivery on your next order if you place it within the next XX days". Time span will vary from business to business as discussed earlier.
- Be worth it to you – it shouldn't wipe all of the profit out of the order.
- Encourage the right behaviour – remember my warning about promotions at the end of the last chapter, and make sure you're using the incentive that will encourage the customer to do what you want them to do as cheaply as possible.

The first thing in the Sequence is the parcel itself and what's in it.

- Can you brand the parcel?
- Can you put a CTA on the delivery paperwork or the despatch note? Most customers read these, so have a clear CTA on there about placing another order.
- Can you put in some marketing materials, like a postcard suggesting they order again? Add in a copy of your catalogue if you have one.
- Can you send them a free and unexpected gift?

This last one can be a great way to push the level of trust they feel up a notch, as it immediately shows you care about their business. You're not just saying it, you're actually rewarding them for it.

Make the free gift something simple, easy to post, and low cost to you, but make sure it also has a high chance of being appreciated by your customers. If you're a tea business, an example might be a branded teaspoon, coaster, or flavour selection pack. The bonus here is that the gift itself is a reminder of your business and an encouragement to buy more!

I noted in an earlier chapter that Blue Chip Wrestling, who make and supply wrestling clothes in America, send a free t-shirt with every order. They source these from t-shirts left over at events they've been to, e.g. "Atlanta October 2013", so the gifts are almost a waste product with little value to the business. To make sure the customer gets a t-shirt they can use, in the checkout they ask for their t-shirt size. Whilst this removes some of the surprise, it does guarantee it will fit!

Think about something you can send out that is practical but rewarding for the customer.

After the parcel has arrived, you can run a sequence of emails (or post/SMSs) thanking them for their first order and asking for the next one. This is also a great time to point out how you value their commitment to you. A Post Purchase Sequence is usually pretty short, but is likely to contain the following:

1. Thank you for your order – this arrives after delivery, explaining how you value them being part of the family. You should include links to social media channels, and if you're running a next order promotion put that in the email too. Focus on CTA and The Conversation.

2. Request for a review – this might come from a different system to your marketing emails, but still make sure it's giving out the right messages. Focus on The Conversation.

3. Big sales message – you could include information on your best sellers, top rated products, or products to progress on to. Focus on CTA.

It doesn't need to be especially complicated or long, because most of the messages you send in this sequence will form part of your regular email broadcast plans.

As you construct your Post Purchase Sequence, remember to utilise the data you gathered earlier about those repeat order windows of opportunity.

Some products deserve post-purchase support (like the Goodbye Crutches example at the start of this chapter) so make sure you prove that you care and provide useful information to the customer.

Other sequences or event-triggered emails

Depending on your customers' repeat buying behaviours, it may be worth setting up some specific sequences to get the next purchase.

Anniversary of First Purchase Campaigns

You may or may not want to mention it's the anniversary, but if you find customers buy your product yearly it's a great idea to automatically email them something to encourage that repeat purchase.

You're About to Run Out Campaigns

If you're selling consumable products that are used regularly, it's a great idea to send an email to remind someone that they're about to run out and it might be time to order again. This works really well for vitamins and toiletries. Look Fantastic (lookfantastic.com) are excellent at this:

Subject line: Is it time to stock up on Kérastase Nutritive Oleo Relax Bain (250ml)?

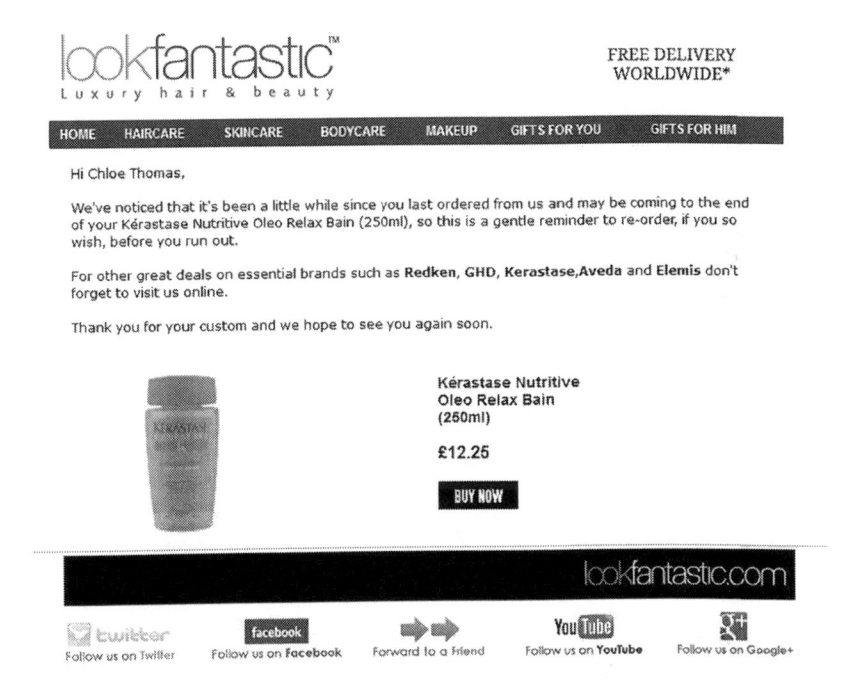

They've successfully featured a product I regularly buy, after the time period that I'm likely to have run out. Another great move was including this line, "For other great deals on essential brands such as Redken, GHD, Kerastase, Aveda and Elemis don't forget to visit us online", which reminds me of their product range and suggests I buy again.

If you don't have consumable products, but you did identify a window of opportunity for getting that repeat order, then use the same tactics to send a reminder during the window of opportunity you spotted.

Reactivation campaigns / "We Miss You"

If you spotted a window of opportunity for turning a First Time Buyer into a Repeat Buyer, then you probably also noticed a drop off after which it's very unlikely you're going to get a second order from that person.

If that's the case, create a Reactivation campaign – this is where just before that end point is reached, you send the customer emails to encourage them to buy from you again. At this point, you almost certainly need to put in an offer or incentive.

Look Fantastic are also very good at this:

Date received	Subject Line	Contents / Offer
13th January	The email above	
24th January	We miss you Chloe	20% off the next order
5th February	We miss you	20% off next order – valid until 8th Feb Free Face mask worth £12 if spend over £55 Free Beauty Collection box worth over £60 if spend over £55 and click on the email link
7th February	Welcome Back Chloe	20% off the next order (same email as on the 24th, just a different subject line)
12th February	We miss you	20% off next order – valid until 15th Feb Free Face mask worth £12 if spend over £55

And it continues – but you get the picture!

When researching for this book, and for other articles, courses, podcasts, and blogs that I create, I'm always surprised by how few businesses have none of these sequences set up. If you set up just one or two of the sequences or triggered email marketing I've outlined here, by my reckoning you'll be ahead of the majority of global retail marketers.

A warning about personalised emails

Be very careful if you're putting personalised data into emails, as it can go wrong. Avoid using it unless you're confident that your data and systems are good and up-to-date. You wouldn't want this happening to you...

The morning before writing the first draft of this chapter, I received this email in my inbox (cropped to hide the perpetrators):

> **Hello Failed prospect,**
> You are invited to the following event:

The following morning, I had a new version sent with the subject line, "Please delete the previous invite sent in error with the wrong information – apologies!". (I don't know about you, but any email that arrives in my inbox with the subject line "please delete" has me searching for the original!)

> **Hello Chloe Thomas,**
> You are invited to the following event:

Isn't it nice when an example falls in your lap just as you need it!

If you do screw up, apologise fast.

Remarketing

As well as marketing sequences to get the second order, you should be considering remarketing to get the second order.

Not all customers will stay subscribed to your emails, and even if they do they might not be bothering to open any of them, so it's important to have other ways of connecting with them.

Remarketing is a great way to do this. As I've briefly touched on in Chapter 5, there are many platforms you can use to do this (Google, Facebook, Twitter and many more sophisticated options). There is a starting point out there for everyone with this.

The common thread in all remarketing is that you are creating a list (or audience) of customers who have performed a similar set of actions (visited your product pages in the last 30 days; or ordered within the last 60 days), and showing marketing to get them to take action. Depending on the remarketing method you're using, how you create the audience will differ, as will where the marketing messages appear.

There are three ways you could be using remarketing to encourage that second purchase.

RLSA

Remember what that stands for? It's a bit of a mouthful – Remarketing Lists for Search Advertising. To kickstart this, create a keyword campaign in Google Adwords that is only to be seen by customers who've bought from you in the past.

Here the audience is created by defining which pages of your website they should have visited, and the marketing messages will appear on the Google Search engine itself.

In this campaign, bid on the big terms that you'd usually be scared of: "gift", "holiday", "flowers", "tea", etc. Hopefully, these will be customers who should be interested in buying their next gift/holiday/flowers/tea from you.

By limiting this keyword bidding to just this audience:

- Your cost-per-click will be lower.
- Your chance of a click-through will be higher.
- Your conversion rate will be higher.

This should all lead to a positive ROI on the activity, and (most importantly) make sure that when your First Time Buyers next want to buy your product, it's your site they come back to.

Dynamic Remarketing

This is where your products are put directly in front of the person.

Here the audience is created by defining which pages of your website they should have visited, and the marketing messages will appear on all kinds of websites. Those marketing messages will be adverts created by Google that show the products the customer is most likely to buy.

If you have enough traffic passing through your website, it can be useful to have those who've previously purchased from you as another audience option for your dynamic remarketing adverts.

You should be able to bid higher and get more traffic from this audience because they are so much more likely to convert.

Remarketing Adverts

As I discussed in the last chapter, you can use both cookie and CRM remarketing to achieve similar ends.

For cookie remarketing the audience is created by defining which pages of your website they should have visited, and the marketing messages will appear on all kinds of websites, if you're using Google, or on Facebook or Twitter if you're using either of those. The marketing messages will be adverts created by you (text & images).

For CRM remarketing, the audience is created from your own customer list (emails and phone numbers) and currently this is only available on Facebook. So you can define the audience in any way you are able to segment your list, and the marketing messages will appear on Facebook. Those marketing messages will be adverts created by you.

The number one way to optimise your remarketing adverts is to segment the data selection. So, you should have a separate set of ad groups for remarketing advertising targeting these customers.

In this Stage:

- For CRM remarketing, use the list of customers who've bought for the first time but not the second. If you have the data volume, and it's worth your effort, consider matching the timespans and messages of your email sequences.

- For cookie remarketing, you can't segment between first time and second time buyers using the basic URL segmentation options. Create a set of marketing that is time bound with the time slots you've identified and, depending on the software you're using, you may be able to do a first time vs. repeat segmentation. If it's worth the time and effort, go for it.

Keep the messaging the same as within the sequences.

Stage 4: Creating Repeat Buyers

Surprisingly few businesses focus enough effort in this Stage, so if you can build a few sequences and get the products right, you'll be way ahead of the competition.

This may feel like a short chapter compared to Stage 1, Stage 2 and Stage 3, and that's because a huge amount of groundwork was done during those three Stages.

As the group of customers you're marketing to becomes better defined (as they move from the left to the right of the model) the marketing becomes easier to identify and implement.

This means (assuming you've done the actions from the previous Stages!) the workload gets a little lighter as you progress further through the Stages, which is great – more revenue per customer you're talking to, greater profit, and somewhat less work to do.

Don't stop yet though – next, you're going to put the icing on the cake with Stage 5.

8 Stage 5: Turning Repeat Buyers into Regular Buyers

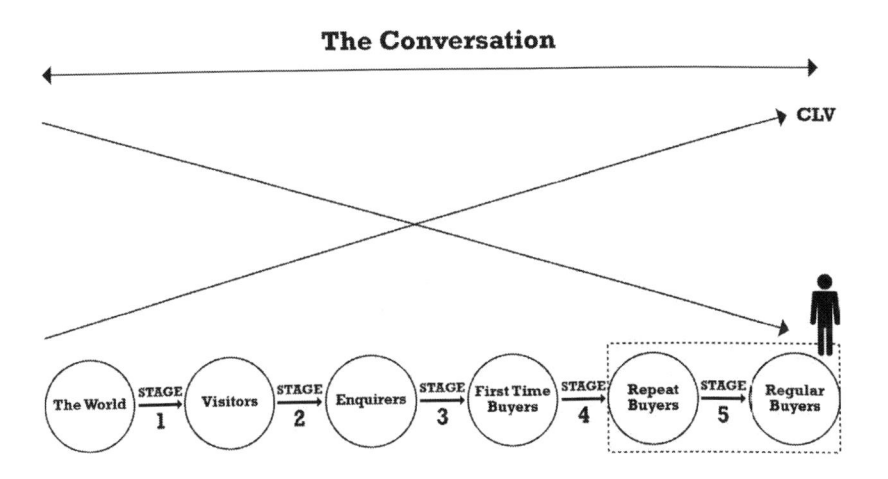

The Conversation

| The World | STAGE 1 | Visitors | STAGE 2 | Enquirers | STAGE 3 | First Time Buyers | STAGE 4 | Repeat Buyers | STAGE 5 | Regular Buyers |

CLV

OUR FINAL Stage. In many ways, this should be the easiest Stage to improve your performance in.

The customers you're talking to have bought from you multiple times, they've experienced your Conversation along their whole journey with you, and it resonates with them (otherwise they wouldn't have bought several times). You are preaching to the converted.

Treat them right and you'll turn them into customers who love you, who care about your success, and they'll forgive minor slip-ups (yup – they'll forgive you).

Treat them right at this point and you have customers for life, whose lifetime value is just going to keep going up, and who are going to help you build your company by providing great feedback and telling other customers about you.

The great majority of steps to achieving Stage 5 success have already been covered. So in this chapter, I'm also going to cover ways you can get the Regular Buyers to help you grow, either by doing your marketing for you or by helping you to learn how to make your business even more attractive.

Basically, you should be leveraging their knowledge and your relationship with them to improve The Conversation and Stage 1 activities!

> Rohan Gilkes from Wet Shave Club sells men's grooming products, primarily via subscription, but they do offer some products as a single purchase. He understood from the start that his existing buyers would be key to his business growth, so he decided to find ways to both:
>
> - Make them feel special and tie them in to his brand.
> - Learn from them to improve the business even further.

> Rohan found a very simple way to do this – once someone places an order on the Wet Shave Club site, they are invited to join a private Facebook Group just for Wet Shave Club customers. Once the buyer gets in there, they have access to exclusive competitions, sneak peaks of upcoming products, and special offers. There's also lots of tribe-relevant discussions. Rohan learns a lot from this and the customers feel more valued. He often takes it up a notch by letting the members of the Facebook Group vote for which products make the next month's box of goodies.[45]

What's the aim of the final Stage?

The aim of the final Stage is to keep your repeat customers buying from you.

It is not about selling them a subscription (see Chapter 2) but it is about keeping subscribed customers signed up.

It's also about treating these great customers in a way that brings even more benefit to your business than just their purchases.

You should make them part of your team – build a community of them, and use that community to:

- Learn more about your customers, what they like, and what they want.
- Learn what they think of your new ideas for products, flavours, colours, routes to market, and marketing materials.

---

[45] You can learn more about how Rohan's building the Wet Shave Club on our podcast, at eCommerceMasterPlan.com/Podcast.

- Turn them into advocates who'll encourage other customers to buy from you – both customers they personally know, and the wider world through their social media and content activity.

The great news is that the more you consult them and ask for their opinion, the more they will buy (so long as you pay attention to what they tell you).

How does The Conversation fit into the final Stage?

The Conversation got these customers to buy multiple times.

Now you can listen to them to understand how you might improve and refine The Conversation to be more powerful and representative of your business.

What can my customers teach me about what I should be doing in the final Stage?

Your actions in this final Stage are all about finding ways to learn more from your customers.

You are not aiming to learn from them about what you should be doing in this final Stage. Instead, you should be focusing on what they can teach you about what you should be doing in Stage 1, Stage 2, Stage 3, and Stage 4.

This actually turns the linear model into more of a heart shape...

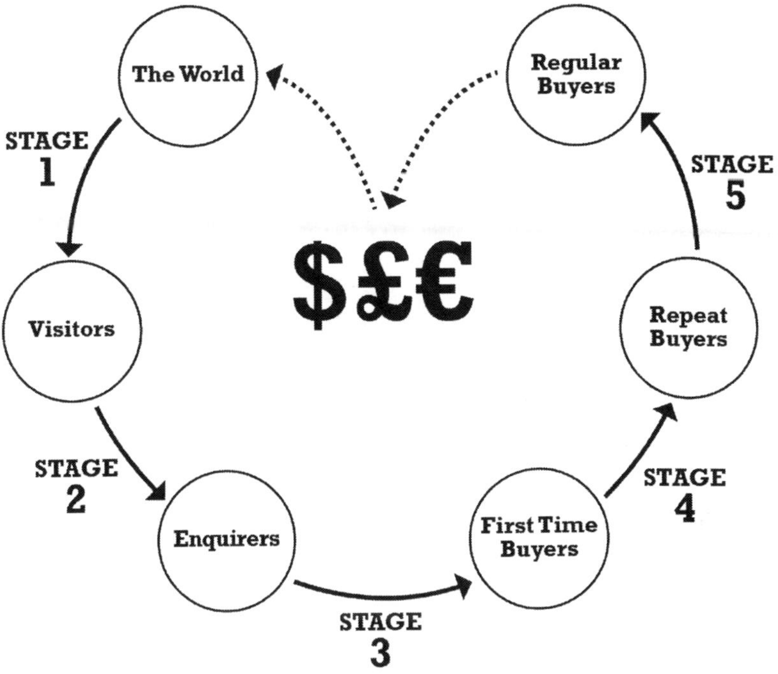
The World
Regular Buyers
STAGE 1
STAGE 5
$£€
Visitors
Repeat Buyers
STAGE 2
Enquirers
First Time Buyers
STAGE 4
STAGE 3

Marketing actions to turn Repeat Buyers into Regular Buyers

We took care of CTAs and marketing to directly drive the next purchase in the last chapter.

In this Stage, it's all about building a community. The more you involve them and the more you make them feel special and important, the more they will buy.

Run a survey

The simplest and least powerful way to learn more from your Repeat Buyers is to send them a survey.

That works for little questions, such as "Would you like to see us branch out from tea into teapots?".

It's not going to help with the more subtle things you could learn, and it's not going to make them feel all that more valued.

Create a community

In the old days, we used to create a "VIP" list and send them slightly different marketing. When I was at Past Times, it included using gold coloured polywrap for their catalogue mailings and offering different discounts.

It did make the customer feel more valued, but it didn't bind them to the business. It was more recognition of how much they spent, and the offers were usually structured to encourage them to spend ever larger amounts.

Here's a selection of ways you can build and use your community.[46]

Dave Rotheroe of Lick My Dip (lickmydip.com) believes the community is so important that he started building his community before he even launched his product. He chose to use a Kickstarter crowdfunding campaign, partly for the seed money but mainly because it would create a group of customers passionate about his business before he even launched.

Bonnie from Miso Tasty sends her regular customers surprise parcels of test products, asking them to try them and send back their feedback.

---

[46] You can hear all about this from Dave, Bonnie, Rohan and Eric in my interviews with each of them at: eCommerceMasterPlan.com/podcast.

The team at Blue Chip Wrestling phone their best customers each month to say hi and see how things are going.

On Rohan's Wet Shave Club private Facebook Group, he asks customers about which products he should stock, regularly posts behind the-scenes information, and encourages them to share their experiences with the products. It's research gold!

Eric Bandholz and the team at Beardbrand in America have a vision to 'change the way society views the beardsman' – it's a calling card that attracts and binds their customers to them. Beardbrands work to create lots of content that will appeal to that customer, such as their recently launched podcast.

At Pact Coffee (pactcoffee.com), they use their fifty top customers to whittle each season's coffee options down to those that will actually be delivered.

If you think it's only smaller companies that can do this, here's a handful of community-building techniques that ASOS are currently using. For those who don't know about ASOS, in 2015 they turned over £1.2bn, making a profit of £48m, and have over 5,000 staff. ASOS's mission is to be "the world's number one fashion destination for 20-somethings" – see how well these examples fit with that target.

ASOS Likes
likes.asos.com

A whole website that's hailed as "Buzzfeed meets Grazia", full of fashion and super-sharable stories such as, "The big debate: are naked selfies a bit of fun or a big mistake?" and "14 ways Paris Fashion Week is giving us school wardrobe nostalgia".

As well as providing the right type of stories and content, the site has a great way to get feedback on what it readers are interested in.

Your feelings?
You can select one or more buttons

HOT	GOALS	OBSESSED	Zzz	VIBES
1	1	3	0	1

#AsSeenOnMe
www.asos.com/discover/as-seen-on-me

Where anyone can share their ASOS inspired looks.

The power of brand advocates

Some, but not all, of your Regular Buyers will become "brand advocates" when they start actively promoting your business to their friends, family, and the wider public via online forums and social media.

This is great news as it means they'll be doing your marketing for you, and because they've been through The Conversation you can be pretty confident that they'll encourage the right sort of customers to visit you and buy from you. A recommendation from a brand advocate can be very powerful: 29% of people say they've been inclined to make a purchase because of a tip from a brand advocate.[47]

---

47 "The UK Customer Service and Support Market", eDigitalResearch iAdvize report, September 2015.

You may even be able to harness your regular customers to help your other customers – 62% of consumers would be willing to engage other website visitors to help them.[48] That could be a customer Q&A area, or a whole forum or just a chat function. Often the best uses of this are in the software space, where the company behind the software create a forum for their customers to help each other out, and their own customer service team only have to get involved occasionally.

The stronger you build that relationship with your Regular Buyers, and the more of them you can recruit, the stronger your business is going to be. That means it will be more profitable and grow faster.

A community does not need to be complicated. Start simple with some surprise gifts, phone calls, or emails and see what happens.

Don't think you have to make anything too complex on day one. You could just start by:

- Sending out a sample pack for feedback.
- Sending a free gift.
- Inviting customers to a sample sale.
- Running a focus group (but please call it something more interesting!).

---

48 "The UK Customer Service and Support Market", eDigitalResearch iAdvize report, September 2015.

Website actions to turn Repeat Buyers into Regular Buyers

This section is about creating a mobile app rather than tweaking your website. Many bigger businesses are using apps to source the community feeling.

You're unlikely to get an Enquirer to download your app, and even if they do it's unlikely to be one of the apps they remember to use. An app creates a very personal relationship between customer and business – often an app feels more trustworthy and personal than a website because it sits right there on the customer's phone. Those emotions can really increase purchase frequency.

ASOS are now getting 44% of their orders via their app. The popularity of the River Island app is giving them service headaches because customers are treating it like Amazon Prime – they buy the shoes over breakfast, the skirt at lunchtime, and the top in the evening!

Consumers spend an average of 30 hours per month in apps, and they are getting increasingly happy with buying via apps. One in every two app users turns to apps to help them make purchase decisions.[49] 67% of tablet and smartphone shoppers only use apps from their favourite stores, but 85% of UK smartphone users do use retail apps.[50] A fifth of them are using their favourites more than once a week.[51]

---

49 "Mobile App Marketing Insights: How Consumers Really Find and Use Your Apps", Think with Google, May 2015.
50 "Mobile shopping: retail usage on the rise", Adobe, 2013.
51 "Retail App Report: The importance of integrating mobile into a retailer's business model", Apadami, Nov 2015.

Before you dive into creating an app...

It's not an easy fix. You can't just turn your website into an app and think that's a job done. You've got to build an app that customers will want to use frequently and keep engaged with (34% of people stop using apps because they've lost interest in them). According to research by Google, attributes associated with frequently used apps include:

- Making life easier (63%).
- Including instructions for using the app (63%).
- Having an appealing design and aesthetic (57%).
- Providing a consistent experience across multiple devices (57%).
- Always providing new content (45%).[52]

Most consumers think there's a gap in the market for more improved retail apps, so very few businesses are getting it right, which means it's not easy![53]

If you're going to do it you also need to avoid getting it wrong first time – 61% of people will stop using a retail app if it's slow, and 26% would think less of the retailer is the app is poorly designed.[54]

Whilst there is clearly a lot to be gained from an app, getting it wrong can have a big negative impact on your business.

---

[52] "Mobile App Marketing Insights: How Consumers Really Find and Use Your Apps", Think with Google, May 2015.

[53] 71% of Brits think that there is a gap in the marketing for more improved retail apps. "Retail App Report: The importance of integrating mobile into a retailer's business model", Apadami, Nov 2015.

[54] "Retail App Report: The importance of integrating mobile into a retailer's business model", Apadami, Nov 2015.

It's a very new area which is changing quickly, and that means you need to be ready to contend with a whole extra world of new issues. Key challenges with retail apps seem to be:

- Keeping up with the technology – tablet users do different things on an app to mobile users, and the technology keeps changing and updating.
- Getting the customers to download it.
- Keeping customers engaged – this might mean personalised content, and getting the balance between incentives and too many alerts is a challenge (40% of consumers said they would delete an app if it sent lots of promotional messages that weren't relevant to them, yet 30% would start using an app again if they were offered a discount to do so).[55]

On the website we have a regularly updated list of good retail apps. You can find it here: eCommerceMasterPlan.com/retail-apps.

Stage 5: Turning Repeat Buyers into Regular Buyers

You've reached the end of The Customer MasterPlan – you've bought Visitors to your website, turned them into Enquirers, then done everything possible to encourage them to buy and buy again.

Then in this Stage, you've looked at how to learn from your best customers and how to make your business better for all your customers. This has the added benefit of making your best customers them feel like a part of the team, which will encourage them to spend more with you.

---

[55] "Retail App Report: The importance of integrating mobile into a retailer's business model", Apadami, Nov 2015.

Stage 5: Turning Repeat Buyers into Regular Buyers | 229

Don't forget to take what you learn from your Regular Buyers back to Stage 1 and use it to improve The Conversation, increasing your conversion rates all through your Customer MasterPlan.

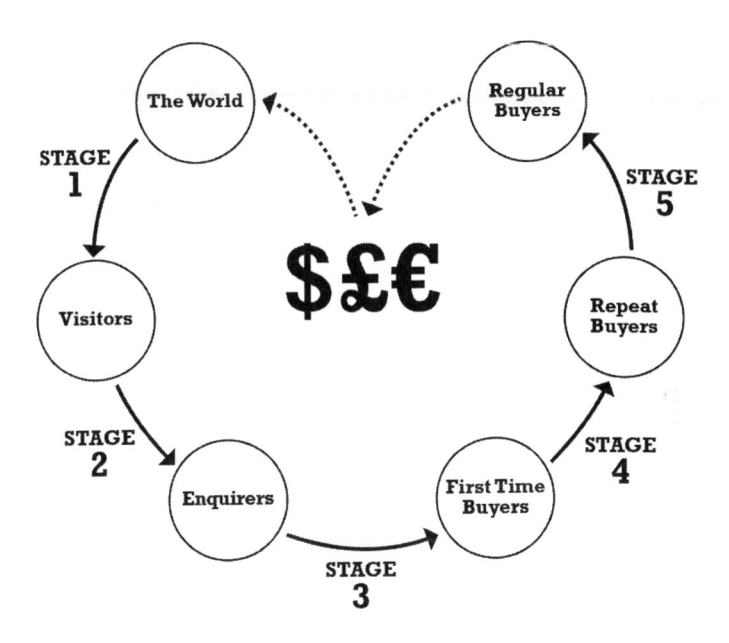

9 Where to Start

CLEARLY YOU'D be crazy to try and work on all five Stages in one go. You would never get anything finished, and more importantly you wouldn't see the benefits for ages.

If you try and implement everything at once, you are going to fail: you're not going to know what's working, and your budget, your time, your effort, your energy, and your inspiration are going to be spread too thinly.

It's really important that before you get excited about improving and building your Customer MasterPlan and your Conversation, you work out which of the Stages you need to focus on first.

As well as looking for the right Stage to get started with, you also need to work out what features of the Stage to start with. The research tasks will help with this. You should also consider what you're already doing, what you enjoy doing, and what you have the skills and technology within the team to improve.

The simple answer to where to start is to identify where the biggest opportunity is (AKA where you're currently performing the worst). But don't think that if the answer is "Stage 1" you're going to do everything possible in Stage 1 before moving on. Rather, you're going to bring Stage 1 up to scratch with the other Stages (maybe improve two things and add one new idea), then reanalyse and move onto the new biggest opportunity, then repeat.

The other complexity to remember is that the work from earlier Stages helps the future Stages! So everything you do to bring in better quality traffic in Stage 1 will increase the likelihood of getting someone right the way through to being a Regular Buyer.

Here are some ideas for working out where to start.

Start-ups

The obvious place to start appears to be work through Stages 1 to 5 in order – as that's where The Conversation starts and ends. If you're a start-up, this is exactly what you should be doing. But don't try to complete everything in each Stage.

- Start by doing a couple of the three categories of marketing in Stage 1.
- Add in an email sign up.
- Work on improving your website's ability to convert a First Time Buyer.
- Set up a simple Welcome Sequence.
- Next put in place a Repeat Purchase Sequence.

Leave Stage 5 out until you've grown much bigger.

Later, analyse your performance (see the information for existing business below) and go back to work on whichever of Stage 1 through to 5 needs your attention.

Established businesses

It's a bit more difficult to work out where to start, but worth putting in the research time in order to see results more quickly.

You may have a burning desire to fix something or start something off as a result of reading the book. In this case, go for it. Get that one out of your system!

Once that's done, you need to take a snapshot of where your business is in order to work out where you should be putting your effort. I'm going to take you through how to take that snapshot. This is a really, really simple snapshot. In every area you can work this out in much more depth, much more precisely, and you're welcome to do that, but what I want to give you in this chapter is a quick and easy way to decide what you should be working on next. This is a simple method you can come back to, again and again, which can be done by every business. Always remember it's more important to start doing something than to get the absolutely perfect analysis.

For example:

- If you already have lots of Regular Buyers then you should really start with Stage 5 in order to work out what got them to you, and buying from you so much – reap the benefits of being able to learn from them before you start reinventing the wheel.

- If you have a huge email list but not many buyers, Stage 3 would be a great place to start. Convert some of those subscribers and earn some cash, so you can invest it in improving the other areas.

- If you're not getting much traffic to your site in the first place, then you need to work on Stage 1 to work out if there is any interest in your product, then sort out Stages 2 and 3 once the traffic builds up.

For this analysis, I'm suggesting you look at the data in three-month blocks to give you plenty to look at. If you feel happier working on full years, or just one month, then go for it. If you're following my lead and going for the three-month blocks of data, I suggest you do it in calendar quarters.

- Quarter 1 = January, February and March
- Quarter 2 = April, May and June
- Quarter 3 = July, August and September
- Quarter 4 = October, November and December

The only real place to benchmark or grade yourself against is yourself, but I'll show some examples at the end of the process to help you work out where your weak spot is.

Stage 1 Performance: Getting Visitors to your website

In Google Analytics, select the last calendar quarter of data and compare it to the total number of sessions in the same period last year, and the previous quarter. This should be really easy to select within the date range tool itself.

Make a note of:

- Sessions this quarter
- Increase in sessions year on year
- Increase in sessions quarter on quarter

Grade yourself out of 5.

Note – if you feel like you've made a lot of changes that have removed some bad quality traffic, then allow for that loss in your grading.

My hints for grading yourself:

- If growth year on year is flat, give a low number.
- If under 10,000, it's also a low number.
- If under 1,000, it's a zero.

Stage 2 Performance: Turning Visitors into Enquirers

Work out how many customers signed up to your email list in the last quarter (use the same time period as you used in Stage 1).

Work out what percentage of site Visitors signed up in that time period by dividing the number of sign ups by the sessions identified in Stage 1.

Make a note of:

- Email sign ups this quarter
- Conversion rate of email sign ups

Grade yourself out of 5.

My hints for grading yourself:

- If conversion rate is over 8%, score a 5.
- If conversion rate is over 5%, score highly.
- If conversion rate is under 1%, it's a score of zero.

Stage 3 Performance: Turning Enquirers into First Time Buyers

To properly analyse Stage 3, you need to consider ALL First Time Buyers, not just those who signed up first. So you're going to take into account leapfroggers!

Take the list of everyone who bought from you in the last quarter and split out a list of those who bought for the first time.

Make a note of how many customers you turned into First Time Buyers in the quarter (customers who bought for the first time).

Grade yourself out of 5.

My hints for grading yourself:

- If the number is higher than your total email sign ups for the same period, score highly.
- If the number is more than 50% of all your orders, score highly.
- If the number is less than 10% of all your orders, score lower.

Stage 4 Performance: Turning First Time Buyers into Repeat Buyers

Take the list of everyone who bought from you in the last quarter, and split out a list of those who bought for a second time.

This may include some of those you've already counted in Stage 3 – that's great! You're converting them to a second purchase really fast!

This may also include some customers who'd made their first purchase before this quarter – again, that's great.

You need to count both types of Repeat Buyers to fully understand the performance.

Make a note of how many people you turned into Repeat Buyers in the quarter (customers who bought for the second time).

Grade yourself out of 5.

My hints for grading yourself:

- If the number is higher than your First Time Buyers for the same period, score highly.
- If the number is less than half of your First Time Buyers for the same period, score lower.

Stage 5 Performance: Turning Repeat Buyers into Regular Buyers

For this model, I'm considering anyone who's bought three or more times to be a Regular Buyer. As you get to understand this model more, you may find that for you a customer is not really a Regular Buyer until they've bought at least five times. This one will vary from business to business, but three and above is a good place to start.

Take the list of everyone who bought from you in the last quarter, and split out a list of those who bought for a third time.

This may include some of those you've already counted in Stage 3 and Stage 4 – once again, that's great! If in one quarter you've managed to get three orders from one person, you're doing a great job!

This may also include some customers who had made their first or second purchases before this quarter – you've guessed it, that's great.

You need to count both types of Regular Buyers to fully understand the performance.

Remember you're counting PEOPLE and not ORDERS. You want to understand how many customers are in this segment, not how many times they bought. So if someone has bought four times in the quarter, they only count as one Regular Buyer. The same is the case for someone who'd placed three orders before this quarter, and one order in this quarter.

Make a note of how many Regular Buyers bought in the quarter (customers who have bought three times or more from you in their lifetime and placed at least one order in the timespan).

Grade yourself out of 5.

My hints for grading yourself:

- If the number is double your Repeat Buyers for the same period, score highly.
- If the number if lower than your Repeat Buyers for the same period, score lower.

Once you've added all this together, you should be able to see which Stage you need to focus on next.

If all your numbers are pretty good but you've not got much traffic, then your focus is going to be getting more Visitors to your website in the first place.

I suggest you make these analyses every quarter, and as you build up the results you'll also be able to see how you're improving in each Stage from quarter to quarter, which will help you make even better decisions about where to focus as the quarters roll by.

Analysing examples

Here are three examples, each with different results, to help you understand how it all fits together.

	Stage 1	Stage 2	Stage 3	Stage 4	Stage 5
Volume:	Sessions this Quarter: 6,000	Email sign ups this Quarter: 300	New First Time Buyers this Quarter: 150	New Repeat Buyers this Quarter: 150	Regular Buyers who bought this Quarter: 100
	YoY Growth: 5% QoQ Growth: 2%	Conversion rate: 5%			
Grade:	1	4	3	3	2

In this example, much of the business is working OK – the email sign ups are coming in and the buyers are moving from Stage 3 to Stage 4. There's a bit of a lack of Regular Buyer orders, but the biggest problem is definitely the traffic.

This business has much of The Customer MasterPlan working, they just need to fill it with customers! For this business, the focus should be on Stage 1.

	Stage 1	Stage 2	Stage 3	Stage 4	Stage 5
Volume:	Sessions this Quarter: 100,000	Email sign ups this Quarter: 1,000	New First Time Buyers this Quarter: 3,000	New Repeat Buyers this Quarter: 500	Regular Buyers who bought this Quarter: 1,000
	YoY Growth: 20% QoQ Growth: 10%	Conversion rate: 1%			
Grade:	4	1	4	1	4

In this example, there are three great Stages and two very poor Stages, both of which score just 1/5.

So which one should you start with? In this case I'd go for Stage 4:

- There are plenty of new customers who qualify for Stage 4. In the last quarter they created 3,000 First Time Buyers, and there's no reason to expect another 3,000 to be created in the coming quarter. If you can convert more of them into Repeat Buyers, it will make a big difference.
- It's clear once this business gets the second order it quickly leads to more orders in Stage 5.
- If Stage 2 is fixed first, it will just create more of the same problem.

	Stage 1	Stage 2	Stage 3	Stage 4	Stage 5
Volume:	Sessions this Quarter: 250,000	Email sign ups this Quarter: 20	New First Time Buyers this Quarter: 500	New Repeat Buyers this Quarter: 600	Regular Buyers who bought this Quarter: 1,000
	YoY Growth: 20% QoQ Growth: 10%	Conversion rate: 0%			
Grade:	4	1	4	4	3

In the final example, the sales are coming in ok, but the email sign-ups are basically non-existent.

There's only one place to start, Stage 2. It should be very straightforward to quickly increase the volume of email sign ups.

That means there'll soon be a problem with Stage 3, so the next thing to do will be to build a Welcome Sequence and improve the conversion to First Time Buyer.

As the volumes increase it may become clear that there's a problem in creating Repeat Buyers as well – so you move onto working on Stage 4, and so it goes on.

Getting started

This book gives you a model for running your business from its start-up stage to whatever you want the end point to be! But simply reading the book isn't going to improve things, you need to start implementing.

Once you've done the analysis outlined in this chapter you'll know where to start, and then you can get into improving the part of your business with the greatest room for it. Once you've got that area up to scratch, run the analysis again and on it goes.

A whole framework for optimising your business Stage by Stage and area by area.

There's number of things available for free on the website to help you with all this:

At eCommerceMasterPlan.com/free, you'll find:

- The template for the analysis spreadsheet
- Workbooks and checklists for each chapter

There are also useful examples of:

- Great retail apps — eCommerceMasterPlan.com/retail-apps
- Great Welcome Sequences— eCommerceMasterPlan.com/welcome-sequences

Please do let me know how you get on (you'll find our contact details on the website), as it's always great to hear how my ideas are working in the real world!

Other assistance

I'm always looking for other ways I can help you make better decisions in your business, be it one-to-one, via online training courses, speaking at conferences, in groups or via the podcast.

To find out what's available right now just head over the website, eCommerceMasterPlan.com

Glossary

Whilst there is a lot of marketing terms in the book, there's just a few I felt deserved to have easy-to-find explanations.

- **AOV aka Average Order Value.** Pretty self-explanatory. This might be calculated over a set period of time, for a customer segment, or a marketing method. It's a very useful way to compare performance.
- **Broadcasts.** These are the emails you send to your whole list on a regular basis. They are all one-offs and are not part of an automated sequence.
- **BSO aka Bright Shiny Objects.** There is a full explanation of this in Chapter 1.
- **CGC aka Customer Generated Content.** Any content that your customers (rather than your company) generates, such as reviews.
- **CLV aka Customer Lifetime Value.** There is a full explanation of this in Chapter 2.
- **CRO aka Conversion Rate Optimisation.** A catch-all phrase covering all the many ways in which you can improve the conversion rate of your website, usually by changing things on the website itself.
- **CTA aka Call To Action.** This is the statement in any piece of marketing or on the website that tells the customer what to do – that calls them to action. It can be as simple as "Buy now" on a button.

- **Demographics.** A way to profile people, usually focused on simple data such as age and gender.

- **PPC aka Pay Per Click.** Any type of online marketing where how much you pay is based on how many clicks you get.

- **Psychographics.** A more complex way to profile people involving lifestyle data such as income, interests and hobbies.

- **RFM aka Recency Frequency Monetary Value.** There is a full explanation of this in Chapter 2.

- **SEO aka Search Engine Optimisation.** Covers the huge of range of things you can do to try and make your website more likely to appear in the search engine results (usually Google).

- **Social Proof.** Often a form of CGC. This could be screengrabs of customers saying nice things about you on social media, or features in newspapers and magazines. Essentially anything that proves other people like your business.

About the Author

Author, international speaker, and host of the eCommerce MasterPlan Podcast.

Chloë Thomas has been working in eCommerce since 2003, learning how to increase orders, up customer retention, and recruit new customers cost effectively, working with businesses from the high-street right down to start-ups. The eCommerce MasterPlan is the result of Chloë's years of experience. The books, blogs and courses have all been created to help eCommerce business owners and marketers to make the right decisions, as they build their own path to eCommerce success. The eCommerce MasterPlan Podcast exists to bring a weekly dose of inspiration directly to the desks of eCommerce business people all over the globe.

Power Retail (Australia) named Chloë as one of the top ten eCommerce commentators in the world, and within six months of launch the podcast was already the top eCommerce podcast in the UK.

Chloë currently lives in rural Cornwall, in the far south west of the UK, and spends a lot of time sipping peppermint tea on the train to and from London. When she's not thinking about eCommerce and marketing, she makes the most of all that's great about Cornwall – the beer, the food, the beaches, the sea, the rugby and, of course, the people.

The eCommerce MasterPlan Podcast

The eCommerce MasterPlan Podcast is available totally for free, via iTunes and other podcast apps – or you can listen directly off the website. You'll find information about all the shows here:

eCommerceMasterPlan.com/podcast

eCommerce Guru Chloe Thomas does it again and over-delivers. ★★★★★
by BOYCEE1 – 13 Jul, 2015

My podcast library is now complete as I have the new podcast from Chloe Thomas subscribed on my phone. She is such a complete guru when it comes to all things eCommerce and as an eCommerce professional myself I have read her books listened to her speaking and now been blown away by her podcast it is definitely filled with nothing but the very best information and advice, thanks for starting a podcast this is the one I have been waiting for the most and you don't disappoint.

Other books by Chloë

This is just the latest in Chloë's series of books about eCommerce strategy and marketing.

They are all available as paperback, audiobook, and ebook, and selling in all the usual places.

eCommerce MasterPlan: Your 3 Steps to Successful Selling

Explains the important theories behind eCommerce success, and maps out the fastest path to success.

eCommerce Marketing: How to get Traffic That Buys to Your Website

Really just does what it says – outlining the 9 key marketing methods you should understand to build your business and how to approach them.

eCommerce Delivery: How your Delivery Strategy can Increase your Sales

Takes you through how to use your Delivery Strategy to your advantage, to increase the chances of getting both the first and repeat purchase.

Find out how to buy at:

eCommerceMasterPlan.com/books

Made in the USA
Charleston, SC
03 October 2016